THE McDONNELL DOUGLAS F-15A/B/C/D/E
EAGLE/STRIKE EAGLE STORY

McDonnell Douglas

The first F-15A (71-280) during roll-out ceremonies at McDonnell Douglas' St. Louis production facility. The "F-15" markings on the nose and tail were unique to this aircraft and the first TF-15A, although smaller versions have been observed on other aircraft.

CREDITS:

The author and **Aerofax, Inc.** would like to thank: C. E. "Bud" Anderson, John Brookes, and Lee J. Whitney, McDonnell Douglas; Mike Binder; Sandee Bright, Martin Marietta; D. Carson, Pratt & Whitney; George Cockle; René Francillon; Jim Goodall; Kelly Green; Wesley B. Henry, Air Force Museum; E. S. "Mule" Holmberg and Kearney Bothwell of Hughes Aircraft Co.; Gayle Lawson; Nancy Lovato, NASA/Dryden; Lois Lovisolo, Grumman; Vincent P. Murone, USAF; Dick Pawloski; Tom Ring; Maj. Brian Rogers, USAF; Mick Roth (special thanks); Lt. Col. Roger Smith, USAF; Keith Snyder; Mike Wagnon; Barbara Wasson; and Jay and Susan Miller.

PROGRAM HISTORY:

During the Korean war, the United States Air Force (USAF) racked up a 7:1 kill-to-loss ratio using North American F-86 *Sabres* against Soviet-built MiG-15s. The overall USAF versus North Korea kill-to-loss ratio was an even more impressive 10:1. The F-86 had first flown during May 1948, and looked every bit a fighter in the tradition of the P-51 *Mustang*. In fact, the *Sabre* was the only U.S. jet aircraft to see significant service that had been designed primarily for aerial combat (albeit, as a fighter-escort), all others having been designed either as fighter-bombers or high-speed interceptors. The F-86 had all the makings of a classic fighter: a high cockpit with a bubble canopy provided excellent visibility for the single pilot, and a large wing resulting in relatively low wing loading (56 lbs. per square foot—only six pounds more than the P-51). These virtues contributed greatly to the outstanding kill ratio achieved in Korea.

Project *Forecast*, a 1963 AF attempt to identify future weapons requirements, foresaw such notable developments as the C-5A and B-1 programs. Directed by Gen. Bernard A. Schriever, commander of the AF Systems Command (AFSC), *Forecast* proved less clairvoyant regarding future fighter programs. It predicted that AF fighter needs in the 1970s and 1980s would be met best by F-111 and F-4 variants "...optimized for the air-superiority role...", and that strategic bombing from aircraft able to fly faster and higher than the enemy would ensure air-superiority. Almost as an afterthought, *Forecast* added that "...the counterair force must be able to destroy aircraft in the air..." And so, American designers got sidetracked from developing true fighters by the magic of radar and electronics. These, coupled with the advent of seemingly workable beyond-visual-range (BVR) missiles, made the traditional "dogfight" appear obsolete. All future battles would be fought without ever seeing the enemy, or so they thought.

The first opportunity to use this new technology, and an entire generation of aircraft built around it, came in Vietnam. It did not work. Not only were the new electronics and missiles unreliable, the entire battle scenario was vastly different from the exercises of the late-1950s and early-1960s. The major problem was that the enemy did not cooperate. During the "war-games", the bad-guys had always approached from one side, the good-guys from the other. All the blips on the radar "over there" were the enemy, and fair game to fire at. The real world didn't work that way since friends and enemies were interspersed in the same air space. To tell the players apart, IFF (Identification, Friend or Foe) systems had to be developed, and deployed—and be dependable. Unfortunately, they too were unreliable, forcing pilots to make visual identification prior to an engagement. These problems with tactics and equipment, coupled with political considerations, conspired against the American fighter pilot and created a rather dismal 2.5:1 AF kill-to-loss ratio in Vietnam. It was increasingly obvious that the fighter-bombers (F-4, F-100, and F-105) and interceptors (F-102, F-104, and F-106) were not destined to be good fighters, and at the time nobody was sure what the F-111 would be capable of (though it ended up being an excellent strike/interdiction aircraft).

On January 7, 1965, Secretary of Defense (SecDef) Robert McNamara allocated $10 million in FY66 funds to modernize the existing tactical aircraft force. At the same time he directed the AF to consider developing a new fighter "...optimized for close air support and useful in ground attack...", and to "assume" tactical air-superiority in all planning. Secretary of the AF (SecAF) Eugene M. Zuckert and Air Staff officials were disturbed by McNamara's instructions to "assume" tactical air-superiority in their planning.

A study entitled "Force Options for Tactical Air" had been initiated during August 1964 under Lt.Col. John W. Bohn, Jr. to critically assess the AF's reliance on high-cost, high-performance tactical fighters. Completed on February 27, 1965, the study found that aircraft such as the F-111 were far too costly to be risked in a limited (i.e., non-nuclear) war and recommended the acquisition of a mix of high- and low-cost aircraft as the most economical method of strengthening the tactical force. For the low-cost role, the study narrowed the candidates to the lightweight, comparatively inexpensive Northrop F-5 and the Vought A-7. Both seemed equally acceptable; the A-7 could carry a greater payload while offering commonality with the Navy, whereas the F-5 had a superior air-to-air combat capability. The AF Chief of Staff, Gen. John P. McConnell, was briefed on the study on March 9, and SecAF Zuckert and his staff were briefed two days later. McConnell subsequently advised Zuckert that the Bohn study clearly showed the folly of "assuming" air-superiority and, in support of this view, cited recent Defense Intelligence Agency estimates declaring the new Soviet interceptors posed a threat beyond the capability of existing U.S. forces to counter.

With this in mind, the AF began studying the basis for a new medium-cost fighter during April 1965. Lt.Gen. James Ferguson, AF Deputy Chief of Staff for R&D, established an Air Staff working group under Brig.Gen. Andrew J. Evens, Jr., Director of Development, and Dr. Charles H. Christenson, science advisor to the R&D deputate. This group conducted prerequisite studies for a Fighter-Experimental (F-X) that would cost between $1-2 million each with a production run of between 800 and 1,000 aircraft. The contemplated fighter would

McDonnell Douglas

F-15 full-scale mock-up differed considerably from production aircraft in having ventral fins, a longer, more pointed radome, and smaller vertical stabilizers. Note gun and missile placement.

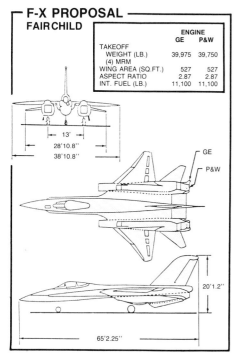

	ENGINE	
	GE	P&W
TAKEOFF WEIGHT (LB.) (4) MRM	39,975	39,750
WING AREA (SQ.FT.)	527	527
ASPECT RATIO	2.87	2.87
INT. FUEL (LB.)	11,100	11,100

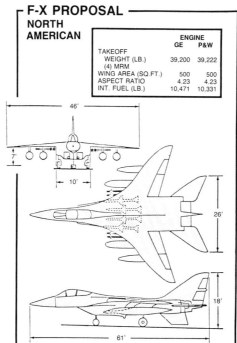

	ENGINE	
	GE	P&W
TAKEOFF WEIGHT (LB.) (4) MRM	39,200	39,222
WING AREA (SQ.FT.)	500	500
ASPECT RATIO	4.23	4.23
INT. FUEL (LB.)	10,471	10,331

possess "...superior air-to-air, all-weather..." capabilities, and was envisioned as a single-seat, twin-engined fighter stressing maneuverability over speed, with an initial operational capability (IOC) date of 1970. As a result of this study, on October 6, 1965, the Tactical Air Command (TAC) released Qualitative Operations Requirement (QOR) 65-14-F outlining the need for a new air-superiority fighter emphasizing an "...aircraft capable of out-performing the enemy in the air..." Other desired fetures included a high thrust-to-weight ratio, an advanced air-to-air radar, a top speed of Mach 2.5, and an armament consisting of infrared short-range and radar-guised BVR missiles.

During the summer and fall of 1965, the AF continued to wrestle with the F-5 versus A-7 issue. The Office of the Secretary of Defense (OSD), particularly Systems Analysis, was still enamored of the "commonality" principle wherein the AF and the Navy would possess a combined tactical force comprised of F-111, F-4, and A-7 aircraft. During July, SecDef McNamara directed OSD and the AF to begin a joint study to select either the F-5 or the A-7 for the close air support role. At the same time, but on a lower priority, he endorsed the AF's work on developing the new F-X fighter. On November 5, the new Secretary of Defense, Dr. Harold Brown, and Gen. McConnell proposed acquiring 11 A-7 squadrons (264 aircraft). Although criticized in some AF circles as a capitulation to the OSD, the decision to buy the A-7 was in fact a sensible compromise that ultimately cleared the way for approval of the F-X, which could now be justified as a "...more sophisticated, higher-performance, aircraft...as an air-superiority replacement for the F-4...."

However, under considerable political pressure, the F-X statement of work was revised to call for an aircraft with the "...best combination of air-to-air and air-to-ground characteristics..." versus the previous QOR-65-14-F air-superiority description. Although this changed the basic character of the aircraft, it did gain enough support in the OSD to allow the AF to launch a major effort to acquire the new fighter.

In response to the revised statement of work, the TAC commander, Gen. Gabriel P. Disosway and his counterparts in USAFE and PACAF issued the first aptly named "12-star letter" (three four-star generals) that stated simply that air-superiority would be severely jeopardized if the F-X were designed to accommodate both air-to-air and air-to-ground missions. They strongly urged the Chief of Staff to endorse air-superiority as the F-X mission. Although the 12-star letters received high-level consideration, Headquarters AF decided to follow the path of least resistance; that is, to continue to study and justify a fighter capable of handling both the air-superiority and ground attack missions.

CONCEPT FORMULATION PHASE

On December 8, 1965 a Request for Proposals (RFP) was released to 13 manufacturers for initial parametric design studies. The RFP specified an aircraft that combined good air-to-air and air-to-ground capabilities, despite the still widely held belief that what really was needed was an air-superiority fighter. Proposals were received from eight companies, and on March 18, 1966 contracts were awarded to Boeing, Lockheed, and North American for a four month Concept Formulation Study. One other company, Grumman, participated in the study on an unfunded basis.

After considering the effects of five variables—avionics, maneuverability, payload, combat radius, and speed—on the F-X in terms of weight and cost, the contractors came up with some 500 proposed designs. To accommodate the dual air-to-air and air-to-ground requirements, the contractors agreed that the F-X needed avionics comparable to the F-111's Mark II system. Moreover, they

understood that multi-purpose meant the use of a variable-sweep wing and that a high-bypass ratio turbofan engine seemed preferable to a low-bypass engine. All of the designs called for armament that included a 20mm M61 cannon with 1,000 rounds, four fuselage-mounted BVR missiles, and a 4,000 lb. external stores allowance. Finally, all the contractor designs favored podded engines over fuselage mounting to avoid the inlet distortion problems encountered on the F-111. The typical design weighed more than 60,000 lbs. and required the use of exotic materials to obtain a top speed of Mach 2.7. The aircraft would have a wing loading of 110 lbs. per square foot, and a thrust-to-weight ratio of 0.75:1. Total R&D costs were estimated at $760 million in FY67-72.

ENERGY MANEUVERABILITY

The AF was not totally satisifed with the results of the study, and did not further pursue the proposals. Since the final RFP had specified an aircraft capable of both air-to-air and air-to-ground operations, what emerged was one optimized for neither. The new commander of AFSC, Gen. Ferguson, and his development planners, Maj.Gen. Glenn A. Kent and Brig.Gen. F. M. Rogers, sensed that the F-X requirements were "...badly spelled out..." They subsequently were able to persuade Gen. Disosway to modify his requirements, thanks in large part to the work of Maj. John R. Boyd. During October 1966, Boyd joined the Tactical Division of the Air Staff Directorate of Requirements and when asked to comment on the just completed F-X proposals, he summarily rejected the designs as inappropriate to the task. A veteran pilot of the late-1950s, and author of an air combat training manual used by the Fighter Weapons School at Nellis AFB, Nevada, Boyd was well qualified to assess fighter aircraft. During 1962, while completing an engineering course at Georgia Tech, he studied the energy changes incurred by an aircraft during flight, and devised a method to measure aircraft maneuverability—the ability to change altitude, airspeed, and direction.

Boyd continued his energy maneuverability (EM) studies at his next assignment at Eglin AFB, Florida, even though his primary billet was as a maintenance officer. At Eglin he met Thomas Christie, a mathematician who also saw promise in the EM theory and who had access to a large, high-speed computer. With Christie's help, Boyd gained access to the computer to confirm his calculations. For this irregularity (i.e., working outside authorized channels) both were severely criticized. But, with the help of Brig.Gen. Allman T. Culbertson, Air Proving Ground Center Vice Commander, Boyd and Christie fought off repeated attempts to terminate their studies and during May 1964 published an official two-volume report on energy maneuverability.

Although the EM theory did not represent anything new in terms of physics or aerodynamics, it permitted planners and developers to compare competing aircraft directly and to demonstrate the effects of design changes on aircraft performance. Applying this method, a model was designed that would demonstrate the effects of specific requirements on the F-X design. By the spring of 1967, through the efforts of Boyd and others, the projected weight of the F-X had been reduced from 60,000+ lbs. to slightly under 40,000 lbs. The proposed engine bypass ratio had been lowered to 1.5, the thrust-to-weight ratio increased to 0.97:1 and the top speed scaled down to a range of 2.3 to 2.5 Mach. Research indicated a wing loading of between 60 to 80 lbs. per square foot would be optimum, and it was planned to use a variable-geometry wing. At this point, total F-X costs were estimated at $7.183 billion, including $615 million for R&D, $4.1 billion for procurement, and $2.468 billion for operations and maintenance over a five-year period. Based on a 1,000 aircraft procurement, the average F-X flyaway cost was computed at $2.84 million per copy.

DOMODADOVO

The F-X formulation phase continued through the spring and summer of 1967. By March a three-part Concept Formulation Package (CFP) and a Technical Development Plan (TDP) were drafted to specify the F-X's rationale, cost and development schedule. Then, during July 1967, the Russians held the famous Domodadovo air show where they introduced six new aircraft types, including the MiG-25 *Foxbat* (at the time thought to be the MiG-23), as well as several new versions of older aircraft. Soon afterwards, the AF submitted the F-X proposal to OSD as the new tactical fighter to replace the F-4. The AF argued for the importance of air-superiority, without which other aerial missions (close air support and inter-

The remotely piloted research vehicle (RPRV) program utilized a 3/8th scale model of the F-15 to explore stall and spin characteristics prior to committing 71-287 to manned evaluations.

diction)[1] would either be too costly or impossible to conduct. It was noted that although the multi-purpose F-4 was a capable air-to-air fighter, its continued effectiveness was doubtful in view of the new, advanced Soviet fighters.

This provided an impetus for the AF to solicit bids on August 11, 1967 from seven contractors for a second round of studies to refine the F-X concept. There were four main topics of discussion: validating performance in the wind tunnel; matching propulsion requirements to achieve the desired performance, including maneuverability; refining avionics and armament (missile, or guns, or both); and determining crew size (1 or 2). Contracts were awarded to General Dynamics and McDonnell Douglas on December 1, 1967 with four other companies, Fairchild-Republic, Grumman, Lockheed, and North American, participating with company funds. The study concluded during June 1968, and the results were reviewed by an AF team that analyzed the results and used them to rewrite the F-X Concept Formulation Package. More than 100 people participated in the review which was headed by Col. Robert P. Daly. The basic airframe issues were resolved quickly, but the composition of the avionics suite caused considerable disagreement. Specifically, the multi-purpose advocates attempted to retain such items as terrain-following radar and blind-bombing capabilities. They argued that future advances in technology would permit weight reductions acceptable to the F-X, but overlooked the costs and risks involved. This review was only partially successful, since many high-risk, high-cost items remained in the baseline.

Several significant events occurred during 1968 that helped shape the course of the F-X program. The Navy had become disenchanted with its version of the joint TFX (F-111B) program, and had initiated the study and development of the VFAX/VFX/F-14. Also, the Presidential elections during November guaranteed a change in the civilian leadership, both in the White House and the Pentagon. Since the Department of Defense still favored the concept of ''common'' hardware, the AF decided to make the requirements for the F-X sufficiently different from the Navy's VFX to justify continued development. And, in an effort to get far enough along in development to protect the program from cancellation by the new administration, the AF decided to skip the prototype phase and proceed directly to full-scale development. The first true requirement for the F-X came during February 1968 when TAC's Gen. Disosway issued ROC-9-68 (Required Operational Capability), which was a restatement of the original air-superiority QOR-65-14-F. During May 1968, AF Chief of Staff, Gen. McConnell, assigned the F-X as the AF's top priority development program.

During August 1968, the Air Staff issued a supplement to the CFP that not only updated the original, but also recommended some fundamental changes. For example, there no longer remained any ambiguities over the AF's air-superiority doctrine:

''. . . it is sometimes held that air combat of the future will assume an entirely different complexion than that of the past. The AF does not share that contention. To the contrary, tactical applications of air-superiority forces will remain essentially the same of the foreseeable future.''

It further noted that the war in Vietnam had taught that smaller-sized aircraft could better escape radar and visual detection. The wing planform remained an open issue, although the ''representative F-X'' described a swing-wing rather than a fixed-wing design. The major subsystems—engine, radar, and weapons—would be selected on a competitive prototype basis, to reduce potential risks. Cost estimates in the supplement included $1.162 billion for R&D and a 635 unit production buy at a flyaway cost of $4.68 million per aircraft.

The final task in the concept formulation phase was the preparation of an F-X Development Concept Paper (DCP). This described the F-X as a ''. . . single-seat, twin-engine aircraft featuring excellent pilot visibility, with internal fuel sized for a 260 nm design mission, and . . . a balanced combination of standoff (missile) and close-in (gun) target kill potential.'' The decision to include just one crew member was arrived at as much to differentiate the aircraft from the Navy's VFX as to save the estimated 5,000 lbs. in additional structure and systems. The twin-engine design was selected because it featured faster

Counterair (air-superiority) operations are intended to achieve and maintain air superiority and, if possible, eliminate enemy air interference. Interdiction involves the reduction or elimination of support for enemy ground forces by destroying his installations and disrupting his communications. Close Air Support seeks to provide fire support to friendly ground forces engaged in combat with the enemy.

F-X PROPOSAL
McDONNELL DOUGLAS

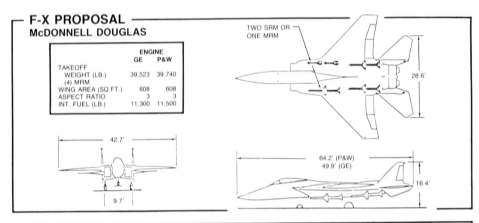

	ENGINE	
	GE	P&W
TAKEOFF WEIGHT (LB.) (4) MRM	39,523	39,740
WING AREA (SQ.FT.)	608	608
ASPECT RATIO	3	3
INT. FUEL (LB.)	11,300	11,500

RF-15 PROPOSAL
(CIRCA 1972)

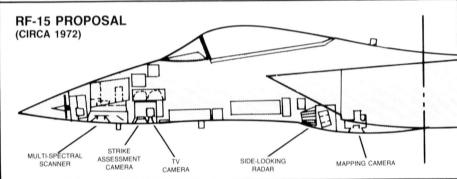

throttle response and earlier availability (interestingly, safety does not seem to have been a factor). The DCP estimated expenditures at $1.078 billion for R&D and a flyaway cost of $5.3 million per aircraft based on a 520 unit production run.

In a letter dated September 12, 1968, Aeronautical Systems Division (ASD) Director of Engineering Standards, R. F. Semler, requested a designation for the new fighter. The Navy had earlier rejected the next available fighter designation (F-13) in favor of F-14 for the VFX. With superstition apparently also influencing the AF, Semler also declined the F-13 designation and requested F-15 instead.

DISSENSION WITHIN THE AIR FORCE

Not all in the AF agreed that the F-15 was the aircraft to buy. One proposed alternative, dubbed the F-XX, was designed by Pierre M. Sprey of OSD Systems Analysis during July 1968. He believed that the F-15 was too expensive, incorporated too much high-risk technology, was unnecessarily complex, and would not achieve its advertised air superiority performance, a view shared by Boyd. Sprey's alternative was a 25,000 lb., single-seat, single-engine fighter designed specifically to fight in the sub/transonic region. It employed a fixed-wing planform and carried an internal gun and two Sidewinder missiles. Sprey's F-XX proposal shunned complex avionics, featuring instead a simple visual radar, easy and inexpensive maintenance, and a unit cost of only $2 million. The proposal also included a VFXX version for the Navy.

The AF and Navy were not impressed. They cited the short, unhappy experience of similarly equipped F-104s in Vietnam, and the limitations of the F-5, as examples of the inadequacy of lightweight fighters. But Sprey and Boyd were not alone in advocating lightweight fighters.

Indeed, many experienced AF and Navy fighter pilots recommended that the best solution to the air-superiority problem was to ''. . . buy MiG-21s!''. Simulations and flight tests during 1968 (including projects Feather Duster and Have Doughnut) demonstrated the superior maneuverability of a lightweight fighter against F-4Es. Although the idea had considerable merit, and was later adopted in the YF-16/YF-17 concepts, it was ill-timed. The F-14 and F-15 projects were too far along to be sidetracked, and all the proposal succeeded in doing was uniting the AF behind the F-15.

CONTRACT DEFINITION

An RFP was released on September 30, 1968 to eight companies: McDonnell Douglas, North American, Grumman, General Dynamics, Lockheed, Northrop, Fairchild-Republic, and Boeing. Only four of the companies submitted proposals, and on December 30 three of them, McDonnell Douglas, North American, and Fairchild-Republic, were awarded $15.4 million contracts for the Contract Definition Phase. General Dynamics was eliminated early during the evaluation process, but the AF was unable to further trim the competition to the previously planned two contestants. The technical proposals were due on June 30, 1969, with projected costs and schedules to follow two months later. The RFP gave the particulars for what the AF was looking for:

- A wing with low loading and optimized for buffet free performance at 0.9 Mach
- A high thrust-to-weight ratio
- A long ferry range, i.e.; to Europe without aerial refueling
- A one man cockpit and weapon system
- A fatigue life of 4,000 flight hours under normal fighter operations

Prototype No. 6 (71-285) was named ''Killer'' and was used in early weapon systems trials. Note kill marks under canopy area denoting QF-86, QF-102, and BQM-34 drone kills.

The eighth prototype F-15A, 71-0287, was the fuel system and spin test aircraft. During the latter program it was equipped with a canistered anti-spin chute.

Several of the early F-15s have been repainted similar to 71-289. The trim is royal blue applied over gloss white.

First TF-15A (71-290) at Edwards AFB. The canopy trim is dark red. Note photo-reference markings around aft AIM-7.

The first F-15B under conversion into the STOL/Maneuver Technology Demonstrator. Note two-dimensional nozzle on left engine.

- A low maintenance man hours per flight hour ratio of 11.3:1
- 360 degree visibility from the cockpit
- Self-contained engine starting with no ground support equipment required
- A maximum gross take-off weight of 40,000 lbs. for the air-superiority mission
- A maximum speed of Mach 2.5
- A long range pulse-Doppler radar with look-down/shoot-down capability
- Low development risk

The proposals were reviewed by the F-15 System Program Office (SPO) which had been organized within the ASD at Wright-Patterson during August 1966 with a charter to oversee both the F-X (F-15) and A-X (A-9/A-10) programs. When the priority for the F-X was raised during May 1968, the A-X project was transferred to a different office, leaving the F-X SPO free to concentrate on the F-15. During July 1969 Brig.Gen. designee Benjamin N. Bellis became the director of the F-15 SPO. Bellis had made a reputation in the development field with the *Matador* and *Atlas* missiles, and later managed the F-12/SR-71 development project. In addition, he had written several AF management regulations and earned advanced degrees in aeronautical engineering and business administration. On October 19 the F-15 office became a "super SPO" when Bellis was named Deputy for F-15. In reporting directly to the AFSC commander, he bypassed the entire ASD, which remained responsible for providing administrative support only. The SPO would eventually absorb the Joint Engine Project Office (JEPO) that was responsible for developing the F-14B/F-15 powerplant, further concentrating the decision making power.

One of Bellis' functions was to chair the Source Selection Evaluation Board (SSEB) that evaluated the three proposals. Eighty-seven separate factors under four major categories (technology, logistics, operations, and management) were considered, and the SSEB's ratings were forwarded, without recommendation, to the Source Selection Advisory Council (SSAC). The commander of the AFSC, Maj.Gen. Lee V. Cossick, chaired the SSAC and this group used a set of weighting factors and evaluation criteria that had been established on June 2, 1969 to evaluate the SSEB's ratings. All of this data, along with the SSAC's recommendation, was forwarded to the new Secretary of the Air Force, Robert C. Seamans, Jr.

At the beginning of December 1969, Representative Otis Pike (D, NY) charged that the AF had violated the Air Corps Act of 1926 by witholding the weighting factors from the contractors. SecAF Seamans explained that the act *allowed* disclosure of the factors, but that such action was "...in no sense mandatory...", and that the act itself was obsolete. The AF's position was later vindicated by the General Accounting Office (GAO) which found itself in full agreement with the AF on the interpretation of the 1926 Act. There were no appeals to the eventual decision, and in fact, Fairchild-Hiller's (Republic's parent company) President, Edward J. Uhl, endorsed the AF's handling of the F-15 competition as having "...been conducted in a most professional manner and...fairly run."

CONTRACT AWARD

The SecAF announced the award of the F-15 contract to the McDonnell Aircraft Company (McAir) division of McDonnell Douglas Corporation on December 23, 1969. The design McDonnell submitted (model number 199-B) was the result of 2.5 million manhours of effort that had culminated in a 37,500 page proposal. The McAir proposal, and subsequent development effort, was led by F-15 General Manager Donald Malvern. The head of the McAir design staff was George Graff, with significant assistance from Bob Little, engineer and former chief test pilot. The contract which McAir received was a significant modification of the total package procurement policy that had received so much criticism in the Lockheed C-5A *Galaxy* program.

The terms, conditions, and restrictions of contract number AF33(657)-70-0300 were spelled out in a 146 page document that was signed on January 2, 1970. It combined a cost-plus-incentive-fee (CPIF) with a fixed-price-incentive-with-successive-target (FPIS) arrangement which had three major items. The first item, which was the only CPIF portion, covered engineering and design of the aircraft; aerospace ground equipment and tooling; Category I flight testing; contractor support for Category II flight testing; plus structural, fatigue, and other pertinent testing. This item had a target cost of $588

Grumman's entry in the F-X competition was the variable-geometry design 399. This design shows many attributes, such as the widely spaced engines and sharply raked air intakes, that would also be found on the VFX (F-14).

million and a maximum 8% ($47 million) incentive fee. The first FPIS item included the production of 20 Category I and II test aircraft, plus spares and ground support equipment (GSE) and three static-test airframes, with a target cost of $469 million and a $42 million (9%) incentive fee. The not-to-exceed ceiling price on the first wing of production aircraft was $937 million, or 145% of the target cost. There originally were not-to-exceed ceiling options on the second and third wings of production aircraft, but between inflation and constantly changing AF production requirements, these options ended up being renegotiated yearly.

Special provisions of the contract included: the "demonstrated milestone" clause, which required a technical demonstration to confirm the feasibility of the design before large sums of production money were committed; and the "total system performance responsibility" clause, which placed responsibility on McDonnell Douglas for satisfactory integration of the engines and all other government furnished equipment (GFE). The contract also specified that McAir was responsible for correcting deficiencies, without any price adjustments. These clauses were included in a successful attempt to preclude the massive failings of the F-111 and C-5A contracts. The AF could decide unilaterally whether McAir had met the commitments, and could delay funding or cancel the program if it desired. The contract also provided for more visible accounting methods, and required McAir to give 17 months notice if it thought additional development funds would be required (17 months corresponds to the government's budget cycle).

Initial planning centered on the eventual production of 749 aircraft: 432 to equip three 72-plane TAC wings, two 72-plane USAFE wings and one 72-plane PACAF wing; 108 for transition training and proficiency; 54 for command support; 12 Category I test aircraft for continued testing; and 143 aircraft for attrition. It was planned that the eight Category II test aircraft would be brought up to operational configuration (as of 1989, the distribution is more-or-less the same, with the exception that one Alaska Air Command and five Fighter Interceptor Squadrons have been substituted for the second USAFE wing and the eight Category II test aircraft were not updated). In addition to the original 749 aircraft, the AF currently plans to procure 392 F-15E dual-mode fighters to equip strike/interdiction squadrons.

NEW WEAPONS

It was decided early during conceptual development that the new fighter would employ a cannon and short-range missiles as its primary armament. Several studies indicated that a new cannon, using caseless ammunition, could be developed that would significantly improve the F-15's kill probability, despite the caseless technical problems previously encountered by the Army. During mid-1968 contracts were awarded to General Electric and Philco-Ford for the development of a caseless ammunition 25mm cannon. The perceived benefits were a faster, less complicated, firing cycle since there were no empty cases to remove, and the ability to carry more rounds for a given amount of weight.

During an evaluation at Eglin AFB from July to October 1971, each contractor fired approximately 10,000 rounds from a prototype cannon. Philco-Ford was announced the winner and began detailed development of the GAU-7A cannon on December 21, 1971 with a $36,181,418 three-year contract for 10 cannon and 160,000 rounds of ammunition. The caseless ammunition for the Philco-Ford design was developed and produced by Brunswick Corporation of Sugar Grove, Virginia.

Unfortunately, technical problems with the ammunition and attendant cost overruns caused the AF to abandon the project during November 1971. Subsequently the GE M61A1 *Vulcan* 20mm cannon was selected as the F-15's internal armament, although provisions for the 25mm cannon remain extant in all airframes except the F-15E.

Missiles have not enjoyed a good reputation among fighter pilots, and the reason is that they have not worked as advertised. During use in Southeast Asia, only 18% of the AIM-9s fired hit their targets, while the success rate for the AIM-7 was even worse, at 9%. During March 1970, General Dynamics, Philco-Ford, and Hughes received contracts for the development of the XAIM-82A short-range dogfight missile to arm the F-15 and other aircraft. By September, rising costs, political pressures, and budgetary restrictions had forced the AF to cancel the contracts and fall back to the *Sidewinder* and *Sparrow III*. As late as 1980, a study released by the Defense Department concluded that the single-shot kill probability of the AIM-9 was 50% and that of the AIM-7 was 35%

McDonnell Douglas

STOL demonstrator first flew with the two-dimensional nozzles on May 10, 1989 with Larry Walker at the controls. The nozzles can vector thrust ± 20° from the longitudinal axis and can also be used inflight as thrust reversers.

when in Navy service, and only 28% for both types in AF service. The lower AF figure probably reflects the smaller and more agile targets the AF expects to meet in combat.

Starting during March 1970, NASA conducted an early independent laboratory evaluation of the McAir design. NASA found the F-15's subsonic drag level to be higher than predicted. To correct this, designers removed the ventral fins and enlarged the vertical fins, along with a significant alteration of their shape. These changes produced the desired drag level improvements and also slightly enhanced stability.

The F-15 passed its preliminary design review (PDR) during September 1970, and the airframe critical design review (CDR) was accomplished successfully during April 1971. Changes from the original F-X design presented during the CDR included: increased height and area for the vertical fins and deletion of the ventral fins (as a result of the NASA study); horizontal tail surfaces and wings moved aft five inches to improve aircraft balance; redesign of the engine air intakes with cowl fences on the upper outer edge and a new cowl lip; and a more symmetrical nose radome to enhance radar performance. It was stated that the airframe would comprise 35.3% aluminum, 26.7% titanium, and 37.8% composites and other materials. The CDR package proposed an initial production rate of one aircraft bimonthly, increasing to one aircraft per month as the production staff acquired the necessary skills and experience to step-up to that rate with no increase in hours worked. It was planned to step-up to a maximum producton rate of 12 aircraft per month. Structural testing of major subassemblies began during November 1971, with the first aircraft scheduled for roll-out during June 1972.

CONGRESSIONAL REVIEWS

Congress began to take several long looks at both the F-14 and F-15 programs during 1971 with the goal of eliminating one of them to save money. The aircraft were compared against each other and also against the MiG-25. Admiral Thomas Moore, Chief of Naval Operations and Gen. McConnell, agreed to present a unified view to Congress that the two aircraft were designed for different missions (fleet defense versus air-superiority). Nevertheless, several alternatives to the F-14/F-15 were proposed, including acceptance of one type by both services, or limited procurement of each, augmented by purchases of cheaper, less capable, lightweight fighters. Criticism of the F-15 also prodded the AF to look at other aircraft. Among the more interesting alternatives was a study by Lockheed's C. L. "Kelly" Johnson that combined the speed of the F-12 with the maneuverability of the F-15. Eventually it was decided that the cost of developing such an aircraft would be prohibitive.

Fortunately for the F-15, development was more or less on track, and the only significant cost overrun (the engine) could be blamed on the Navy. However, the AF did agree to undertake the development of two lightweight fighter prototypes. Out of this program emerged the General Dynamics YF-16 and Northrop YF-17. These fighters were very reminiscent of the aircraft proposed by Pierre Sprey during 1968 and would prove to be nearly equal to the F-15 in terms of performance while being substantially less expensive. The YF-16 was subsequently selected for further development, and has enjoyed a healthy production run despite a forced diversion away from its lightweight fighter origins (i.e., more weapons, radar, avionics, etc.).

During February 1972, SecAF Seamans placed the in-

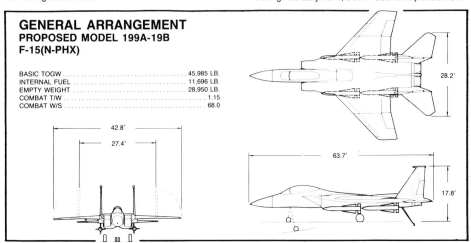

GENERAL ARRANGEMENT
PROPOSED MODEL 199A-19B
F-15(N-PHX)

BASIC TOGW . . . . 45,985 LB.
INTERNAL FUEL . . . . 11,696 LB.
EMPTY WEIGHT . . . . 28,950 LB.
COMBAT T/W 1.15
COMBAT W/S 68.0

28.2'

42.8'

27.4'

63.7'

17.8'

The second TF-15A (71-291) on an early test flight in air-superiority blue with da-glo orange trim. Note early development model FAST Packs along engine nacelle trunks.

71-291 later was painted overall blue again, and incorporated an unpainted metal nose with a long instrumentation boom. ''F-15'' markings on nose and tail are noteworthy.

71-291 in overall air-superiority blue on an early air-to-ground demonstration flight. Aircraft is carrying 18-500 lb. bombs. Note M61A1 20mm cannon port is faired over.

71-291 was used for demonstrations to the Armée de l'Air during 1976 and was overall blue with French AF markings. Note fourteen flag emblems under forward cockpit.

71-291 was used by McAir as a demonstrator during 1976 and was painted in this Bicentennial red, white, and blue scheme developed for use by the ''Thunderbirds''.

Still in red, white, and blue, 71-291 went on a ''world tour'' during 1977 with slightly modified markings on tail and FAST Packs. Note AIM-7 attach points on FAST Packs.

71-291 was repainted in ''Compass Ghost'' for her role as the Advanced Fighter Capability Demonstrator (AFCD). Note advanced fire control pod on centerline station.

With a load of air-to-ground weapons, 71-291 shows the ''European One'' camouflage used on the ''Strike Eagle'' demonstrator. Note GEPOD 30 mm cannon on centerline.

crease at $532 million in overall engine program costs, including procurement. To circumvent the increased costs to some extent, the equipment list for the F-15 was pared back during early 1972, eliminating the planned multi-sensor display, the moving map display, the helmet mounted sight and the Target Identification System, Electro Optical (TISEO). The planned vertical tape-style instrumentation also was eliminated in favor of less-expensive conventional round dials. Several other items including the bird-proof windshield were considered for elimination, but subsequently reinstated. Thought also was given to using the ejection seat from the F-105, but a new seat was developed anyway. The omitted equipment, particularly the long-range optics, would hamper the eventual operational use of the F-15.

NEW RADAR

During August 1968, the AF awarded contracts to Westinghouse and Hughes for the development and testing of a new X-band pulse-Doppler radar set for the F-X fighter. During the initial analysis for the new system, the following configurations were considered:

1. Radar for ranging, an optical computing sight, and a dive-bombing capability utilizing a depressed reticle.
2. As above, plus a tracking radar for all-weather capability against airborne targets and semi-active guidance for *Sparrow III* air-to-air missiles.
3. As above, plus expansion of the tracking radar to allow detection of low flying targets and a heads-up display for aerial combat.
4. As above, with expanded radar and on-board computers to provide a degree of capability against ground targets. In addition, provisions were allocated for an optical means of identifying distant airborne targets (TISEO).
5. The most complex configuration, with a multi-purpose radar suitable for blind bombing and aerial combat, as well as all the capabilities listed above.

In the final analysis, the fourth option was chosen, with the radar possessing a ''look-down/shoot-down'' feature that would allow the detection and tracking of targets among ground clutter. The fifth option eventually would evolve into the system installed in the F-15E *Strike Eagle*. After the award for the F-15 contract, McDonnell Douglas was given the responsibility for the selection of the winning radar, subject to AF approval. During 1970, the two competing systems were installed in test aircraft for airborne trials, with Hughes using a Douglas WB-66D (55-391) with an F-15 radome attached to the nose. During October 1970, McDonnell Douglas awarded Hughes an $82 million contract for the design, development, and testing of the new long-range, lightweight radar.

On October 12, 1973, a 3/8th scale model of the F-15 was dropped from a NASA NB-52 from 45,000 ft. at 175 knots, initiating a unique flight test series. The model was controlled from a ground station at the Dryden Flight Research Center at Edwards AFB by NASA pilot Einar K. Enevoldson. The flight lasted approximately eight minutes, and the model was recovered by a Navy helicopter at approximately 15,000 ft. G. P. Layton was the NASA program manager for the remotely piloted research vehicle (RPRV) project which was developed to explore the F-15's stall and spin characteristics prior to the upcoming flight test program. Three models were built, the third having a more refined flight control system. The models were constructed by McAir out of aluminum and fiberglass and were 23.8 ft. long, had a 16.0 wingspan, weighed roughly 2,000 lbs, and were unpowered.

ROLLOUT

The first F-15A-1-MC (71-280) was rolled out of McAir's St. Louis plant on June 26, 1972. At that point, the program essentially was on schedule, with costs cited to be below target (in contrast to the significant cost overruns and schedule slips so obvious on the F-111 and C-5A programs). Although the airframe and avionics efforts were on schedule, Pratt & Whitney still was running behind on both deliveries and testing. Total funding for the F-15 program through FY69 had amounted to $77.5 million, with $174.9 million in FY70, $349.5 million in FY71, $420.2 million in FY72, and $454.5 million in FY73 allocated to research and development, and an additional $421.6 million in FY73 allocated for the first 30 operational aircraft.

During July 1972, allegations were made on the Senate floor that the F-15 program was concealing some significant problems, including: a tendency to spin; cross-wind landing problems; a radical yawing of the aircraft when the M61 cannon was fired; and a high failure rate of the F100 engine. Only the crosswind landing charge would

find fact during flight tests, and that was overcome easily by modifying the main landing gear struts. The engine was indeed having problems completing the required testing, but these were documented and understood, and modifications already were underway.

After rollout in St. Louis, the first F-15A was disassembled partially and shipped to Edwards AFB in a Lockheed C-5A transport. There it was reassembled and following systems testing, made a 50 min. first flight beginning at 0821 PDT on July 27, 1972 with McAir chief test pilot Irving L. Burrows at the controls. During this flight the aircraft reached 12,000 ft. and 320 mph. Within the first week, the prototype had made four additional flights, totalling 4 hrs. and 48 min. at speeds up to Mach 1.5 and 45,000 ft. During the following two months, Irv Burrows and Peter Garrison accumulated over 40 hrs. in 71-280. Flight number 1,000 was accomplished during August 1973, by which time the F-15 had flown above 60,000 ft. and at speeds in excess of Mach 2.5.

Of the initial 20 aircraft, 12 (71-280/291) were dedicated to Category I Contractor Development, Test and Evaluation (CDT&E) testing, and eight (72-113/120) were allocated to Category II AF Development, Test and Evaluation (AFDT&E). Category II testing began on March 14, 1974, although the AF had already been flying approximately 15% of the Category I flights on an unofficial basis. The test organization was known as the F-15 Joint Test Force (JTF), and its director, Col. Wendall H. Shawler, became the first AF pilot to fly the new fighter. The JTF was made up of 13 pilots, seven from TAC and six from the AFSC. The unit later changed its title to F-15 Combined Test Force, and as of mid-1989 continues to support F-15 flight testing. Category III was the Follow-On Test and Evaluation (FOT&E), initially conducted by the AF Test and Evaluation Center, and later by the 433rd Fighter Weapons Squadron (FWS) at Nellis AFB.

Experience from previous programs had indicated to the AF that some 20% (4 aircraft) of the test aircraft would be lost during the flight test series. In fact, none were lost, resulting in a number of surplus airframes, four of which later were sold to Israel, and one of which was used for project *Streak Eagle*. The test aircraft were assigned McAir numbers based on their production sequence, hence the first F-15A (71-280) was known as F1, the second (71-281) as F2, etc.

The flight test program proceeded smoothly, and slightly ahead of schedule, during the remainder of 1972 and 1973. A severe wing buffeting problem in a small, but critical, part of the envelope (30,000 ft. at 0.9 Mach and 6 g) was discovered early, and engineers at St. Louis tried several fixes, most notably large fences mounted midspan on each wing of 71-289. The final solution was found by engineers at Edwards during March 1974, who somewhat unceremoniously sawed off three square feet of each of 71-283's wings to create the present raked wingtip. The rough edge of the wingtip was filled with wood and wood filler until metal wingtips could be fabricated, and after the fix was verified, the other prototypes were similarly modified. It appears that the first production aircraft (73-108) was the first aircraft fitted with the new wingtips at the factory.

The first three aircraft also suffered from a mild flutter condition that wind tunnel analysis revealed could be corrected by cutting a snag in the horizontal stabilator. Therefore, a 16.5 in. wide section was removed from the inboard four feet of the leading edge of each stabilator causing a minor shift in the center of pressure, which cured the flutter. The new stabilator was a production feature on 71-283, and the first three aircraft were subsequently retrofitted. The original 20 sq. ft. speed brake was required to extend to an almost vertical angle to create the drag required for rapid deceleration, and this caused a buffet condition at some airspeeds. The solution was to enlarge the speed brake to 31.5 sq. ft. and change its contours so that the deployment angles remained more reasonable. The initial production aircraft (73-108) was the first aircraft to incorporate the new speed brake at the factory. Several of the test aircraft were modified to carry the new speed brake, although some were not re-fitted with the new speed brake well, so the speed brake could not close completely.

There was another modification made early in the program that did not result in a change to the aircraft's external appearance. The aircraft, which uses comparatively narrow tracked landing gear (nine feet between the main wheels) and a high AOA (12°) for landing, was not particularly tolerant of cross-winds. An internal modification to the main landing gear struts, and several changes to the flight control system, allowed the F-15 to handle cross-winds up to 30 knots.

All totaled, the F-15 flight test program generated 38 engineering change proposals (ECP), compared to the 135 generated during the F-4 test program. All but two of these were incorporated into the first production aircraft (73-108) and all were incorporated into the third (73-085). All designs seem to increase in weight prior to and during production, with the original F-4 gaining 3,050 lbs. between the first prototype and the first production aircraft. In contrast, the F-15 gained only 188 lbs. And, in fact, between the third production aircraft and the 87th (74-117), weight was down 283 lbs., or 93 lbs. *less* than the first prototype.

The F-15 also was designed from the start to be easier to produce than previous fighters with the use of large one piece forgings instead of building-up many smaller pieces saving considerable production effort. The SPO had planned on 690,000 production hours for the first five prototypes, but McAir completed them in only 466,000. The first production F-15A required 69,000 manufacturing manhours, and an additional 11,000 manhours in final assembly. By contrast, the first production F-4 (the 48th aircraft) had required 589,000 manufacturing manhours and 35,000 manhours in final assembly. An unintentional, but welcome, feature introduced on the F-15 was reduced noise. As measured one mile from the departure end of a runway, the F-15 was 15 decibels quieter than the F-4, and 13 decibels quieter than the F-104.

One of the F-15 contractual requirements was the capability that an engine be changed in less than 30 min. After a fair amount of practice, a highly choreographed McAir team met this requirement by changing a complete engine assembly in 18 min. and 55 sec. on February 12, 1974. The company readily admitted that the average AF unit probably could not duplicate this feat (although, in fact, several have), but the demonstration fulfilled the contract requirement, and proved the F-15 could be quickly serviced.

During the proposal effort that led to the F-15 contract, McDonnell Douglas had investigated the concept of conformal packs to contain fuel and systems without taking up space on the aircraft's weapons stations. This had been in an attempt to fulfill the ''transatlantic'' ferry range required in the RFP. During early-1974 it was decided to build and demonstrate the concept, dubbed ''FAST (Fuel and Sensor Tactical) Pack'', to the AF and other potential customers. The prototype units, built to contain fuel only, were completed just 139 days after the engineering go-ahead. The unit was designed for quick installation on the aircraft and was fitted to the fuselage of the F-15 using the standard USAF bomb lift truck with a simple adapter. Maintenance personnel raise it into position, install two bolts, and make one electrical and two fluid connections. The FAST Packs are not capable of being jettisoned, but the fuel can be dumped through the aircraft's normal dump system. Each FAST Pack provides 114 cu. ft. of space, is 32.5 ft. long, and has a maximum cross-section of 24 in. by 36 in. The *Sparrow* missiles they displace can be carried on the corners of the FAST Pack itself. In addition to fuel, McAir has proposed versions containing reconnaissance equipment, *Wild Weasel* systems, low-level strike equipment, and even one version that incorporated a rocket engine in the back that could be used for thrust augmentation.

The fuel-only version was demonstrated successfully on the second TF-15A (71-291) during a flight on July 27, 1974 and subsequently was purchased by Israel for use on their aircraft. 71-291 demonstrated the concept during September 1974 when it flew 3,063 miles from Loring AFB, Maine, to the Farnborough (England) airshow unrefueled. The aircraft lifted off at 67,000 lbs., including 33,000 lbs. of fuel. Total flight time was 5.4 hrs. at 0.85 Mach with 4,300 lbs. of fuel remaining when it landed at RAF Station Bentwaters. The USAF later decided to equip all F-15C/Ds with the capability to carry conformal fuel tanks (CFT), which is a new name, same equipment, and also specified a modified (tangential carriage) version for the F-15E.

F-15A/B

This was the initial operational configuration, with 383 F-15As and 60 F-15Bs being built, including foreign military sales to Israel. The F-15B is a two-seat version of the F-15A, and was designated TF-15A until October 1978. The inclusion of the second seat and attendant systems increased the aircraft weight by approximately 800 lbs. The two-seater is fully mission capable with the exception of not carrying the Northrop AN/ALQ-135 ECM system which normally is located in the area occupied by the second seat. The first operational aircraft, a TF-15A-7-MC (73-108) was delivered to the 555th TFTS at Luke AFB, Arizona, on November 14, 1974.

McDonnell Douglas

George Cockle

"Streak Eagle" (72-119) is shown with the "Aquila Maxima" badge that was removed before the record attempts. Aircraft was left unpainted to save weight.

The first production F-15A (73-085) was originally air-superiority blue, but is shown here in "Compass Ghost". Note later-style black LA tailcodes.

Mick Roth

Fred Harl

Several aircraft at Luke were painted in high visibility markings for a short time. These are black and white stripes applied on a standard "Compass Ghost" aircraft (73-122).

Two Luke aircraft (73-104 and 73-113) show the white tail codes used only by Luke, Langley, and Nellis. Note dummy fin-tip pods and external stiffener on speedbrake.

The F-15 had a remarkably uneventful flight test program, and its introduction into squadron service also proceeded smoothly. The major problem encountered was with the F100 and a stagnation anomaly which quickly degenerated into a compressor stall, caused primarily by large or quick throttle excursions. Since these were frequently encountered within the normal operating environment of a fighter, they caused considerable concern. P&W did find a partial fix, mainly modifications to the engine control units to smooth out throttle transients, but no complete fix ever was implemented on the F100-PW-100 engines. Other problems which cropped up as a result of the stall/stagnation condition centered around engine fatigue and low engine component life resulting in a significantly lower than expected readiness rate. There are some who believe the variable geometry inlet makes the stall/stagnation/durability problem much more serious on the F-15 than on the fixed inlet F-16. The introduction of the F100-PW-220 engine, with its electronic engine controller, has eliminated a good deal of the stall/stagnation problems, however.

Engine problems not withstanding, not a single F-15 was lost during the flight test program, and the F-15 is the only USAF jet fighter to complete its first 5,000 flight hours without a loss. The first F-15 loss (73-088) occurred on October 15, 1975 after a total of 7,300 hrs. had been accumulated by 47 aircraft. The loss resulted from the pilot turning off both generators because he had smoke in the cockpit, resulting in a temporary loss of power to the fuel boost pumps, causing both engines to flame-out. The emergency generator came on-line, but the aircraft had been on a low level gunnery mission, and was at too low an altitude to effect an air-start; the pilot ejected successfully. The second F-15 loss (74-129) oc-

curred during early 1977 after 177 *Eagles* had accumulated over 30,000 flight hours. The aircraft collided with an aggressor F-5E during a Red Flag exercise at Nellis AFB. In fact, by the end of FY88, the F-15 had logged over 1 million flight hours and was averaging 3.27 major accidents per 100,000 flight hours, compared to its nearest rival, the F-16 at 6.52. This has earned it the distinction of being the safest fighter in the history of the AF. Fifteen years earlier, from 1956 to 1973, the average loss rate for twin-engine fighters was 10.5, while single-engine fighters had lost a staggering 17.1 per 100,000 flight hours (not including combat). The following illustrates some loss rates:

Aircraft Type	20,000 Hours	30,000 Hours	145,000 Hours	
F-100	11	26	--	(USAF only)
F-101	10	12	--	
F-102	10	20	--	
F-104	15	24	--	(USAF only)
F-105	6	8	--	
F-106	4	6	--	
F-111	5	6	14	(USAF only)
F-4	3	9	20	(USAF only)
F-14	3	5	20	(USN only)
F-15	1	1	10	(USAF only)
F-16	4	7	22	(USAF only)

During 1975, several detail changes were introduced as a result of data obtained during project *Streak Eagle*. These included a redesign of the ejection seat handle to accommodate pressure suit gloves more easily, the development of a new control schedule for the variable geometry inlets to improve supersonic performance, and a change in the fuel flow system to help prevent flameouts under low fuel conditions.

During April 1977, McAir proposed raising the F-15 production rate from 9 to 18 aircraft per month during FY78,

and increasing the total number procured by 321. This was an attempt to achieve an economical production rate (something the F-15 never had), thus lowering the unit cost of the *Eagle* and making it competitive with newer, less capable aircraft (i.e.; YF-16, YF-17). At the higher production rate, McAir offered a unit flyaway price of $8.85 million in FY78 dollars, about a 28% decrease from FY77 costs. Unfortunately, the AF was committed to the lightweight fighter concept, and F-15 production rates actually started declining.

A job that never was envisioned when the F-15 was designed was that of satellite killer. During 1979 the AF awarded a contract to the Vought Corporation (LTV) to develop a two-stage low-earth orbit anti-satellite (ASAT) missile. This missile used a first stage derived from a Boeing AGM-69 short-range attack missile (SRAM) and a second stage powered by an Altair III rocket motor. The missile was 17.81 ft. long, weighed approximately 2,700 lbs. and was carried on the centerline pylon with a special launcher. New support equipment carried aboard the aircraft included a back-up battery, a communications link for receiving mid-course guidance, and a dedicated microprocessor. Captive flight trials began during 1983, and the first launch was accomplished on January 21, 1984. Early flights were conducted by an F-15A-17-MC (76-0086) based at Edwards with the flight profile consisting of a zoom-climb to a predetermined point at roughly 80,000 ft. at which point the missile was launched to seek out a point in space using internal guidance.

On September 13, 1985, an F-15A-18-MC (77-0084) from the 6512th Test Squadron at Edwards departed Vandenberg AFB, California, and carried out the successful destruction of an orbiting satellite (*Solwind* P78-1). This trial originally had been planned against a dedicated target satellite, but when this could not be arranged, *Solwind* was chosen as an alternative. Many in the scientific community thought this was unfortunate since *Solwind* was still transmitting data even though it had passed its estimated useful life in orbit. Initial plans called for equipping aircraft of the 48th FIS at Langley AFB and the 318th FIS at McChord AFB, Washington, with the weapon, but Congress since has halted further testing and procurement as a result of political, philosophical, and economic pressure.

The air-superiority configured F-15A has an excellent thrust-to-weight ratio of over 1.45 with half-fuel and four *Sidewinders* and four *Sparrows*. The aircraft has a maximum speed in excess of Mach 2.5, a service ceiling of over 65,000 ft. and has demonstrated a "zoom-climb" ("snap-up") capability to well over 80,000 ft. The only significant shortcoming is a less than optimum fuel fraction. Current thinking is that internal fuel weight expressed as a fraction of take-off weight in the air-superiority mode should be about 0.30 for a modern fighter. The F-15A comes in at 0.28, and as a consequence is a bit short of the desired radius of action. This

Jay Miller/Aerofax, Inc.

The first aircraft delivered to the Tactical Air Command was TF-15A-7-MC 73-108 on November 14, 1974. Note air-superiority blue paint and "TAC 1" moniker on nose. Aircraft did not have tailcodes when delivered.

This F-15A-10-MC (74-081) from the 43rd TFS/21st TFW at Elmendorf AFB is part of the Alaskan Air Command. Markings on inside of vertical stabilizer are noteworthy.

The three training squadrons of the 325th TTW at Tyndal AFB, Florida, fly early model F-15As like 74-113. Training flights are normally made with a centerline external tank.

The 33rd TFW at Eglin AFB, Florida have traded their F-15As (such as 74-115) for MSIP-II F-15Cs. The F-15As were transferred to Air National Guard units.

The 57th FWW has flown almost every model F-15, including this F-15A-12-MC (74-120). Nellis aircraft have also used white tailcodes on occasion.

was one of the major impetuses for the development of the F-15C which carries an additional 2,000 lbs. of fuel.

A Multi-Stage Improvement Program (MSIP-I) for the F-15A/B was developed during 1982 in conjunction with the MSIP-II program for the F-15C/D. During February 1983, MSIP-II was given the production go ahead, but MSIP-I was cancelled as uneconomical. Nevertheless, as F-15As go through depot level maintenance they are receiving many of the modifications originally contained under MSIP-I. These generally are small improvements to systems that enhance their reliability and/or maintainability, and do not significantly alter the capabiltiies of the aircraft.

F-15C/D

The F-15C carries 2,000 lbs. more internal fuel than the F-15A, and also is equipped to carry conformal fuel tanks (CFT). The modification package initially was known as "PEP-2000" (Production Eagle Package). An additional UHF radio, improved ECM gear, a strengthened airframe, and a new ejection seat also were included. The first aircraft (78-0468) made its initial flight on February 26, 1979 at St. Louis and the F-15D (78-0561) two-seat version first flew on June 19, 1979. A total of 408 F-15Cs and 62 F-15Ds were procured for AF service, and an additional 65 F-15Cs and 23 F-15Ds were built for export to Israel and Saudi Arabia (for totals of 473 F-15Cs and 85 F-15Ds). Aircraft number 1,000 (F-15C-38-MC, 84-0030) was delivered on October 3, 1986. The last production F-15C/Ds were ordered during FY86, and it currently is anticipated that with the AF intending to wait for the Advanced Tactical Fighter (ATF—YF-22/YF-23) to come on-line during the early-1990s, no further air-superiority variants will be procured.

Since late-1979 the Hughes AN/APG-63 radar in the F-15C/D has been equipped with a programmable signal processor (PSP), which enables changes to be incorporated in the radar more easily and at less cost. An updated radar data processor increased memory from 24k to 96k words and these added features enabled the radar to operate in a high-resolution "raid assessment" mode which could identify clustered targets individually. The PSP and other radar improvements were flight tested on a F-15A-18-MC (77-0084) during 1984 and 1985 and all F-15Cs delivered without the radar modifications have been retrofitted with them.

Minor changes have been made to the landing gear and tires to allow for the increase in maximum takeoff weight, which now can be as high as 68,000 lbs. with full internal fuel, external tanks, and CFTs. An empty F-15C is about 600 lbs. heavier than an F-15A. The F-15C/D is equipped with an overload warning system which permits the pilot to maneuver safely to the 9 g limit of the airframe at all design gross weights, as opposed to the 7.33 g restriction applied to the F-15A in certain flight regimes.

During February 1983, the AF awarded McDonnell Air-

craft an \$86.7 million contract for initial F-15C/D MSIP-II work, with a further \$274.4 million released during December 1983. This covered the introduction of a Hughes AN/APG-70 radar with PSP memory increased to 960k words and a tripling of processor speed; upgrading the aircraft's central computer with four times the storage (128k words) and triple the speed; replacing the cockpit armament panel with a single Sperry multi-purpose color display (MPCD); new throttle grips and controls; a new video tape recorder split image control panel; and adding provisions for the Joint Tactical Information Distribution System (JTIDS).

Linked to the aircraft's computer, a new Dynamics Control programmable armament control set (PACS) allows the quick integration of future weapons. Additionally, the capability to carry and launch the new AIM-120A AMRAAM has been added. Other MSIP-II improvements include an enhanced electronic countermeasures suite consisting of a Northrop AN/ALQ-13B internal countermeasures system, a Loral AN/ALR-56C radar warning receiver, Tracor AN/ALE-45 chaff/flare dispensers, and a Magnavox AN/ALQ-128 warning system. It is expected that the changes to the electronic systems will result in roughly a 25% improvement in reliability, with a corresponding increase in the readiness rate. Flight testing of the new systems began during December 1984, and the first production F-15C (84-0001) to incorporate the changes was delivered on June 20, 1985.

Although the installation of TISEO on the F-15 was abandoned during 1972, the development of a new generation electro-optic sensor was initiated during 1987. Dubbed "Eagle Eye III" by Perkin-Elmer, this sensor will be mounted in the same left wing root space originally reserved for TISEO. The system consists of a 23 in. long, 10 in. diameter lens assembly and video camera which provides an image on the Sperry video screen used by the armament system. The AF has not announced production plans for the system.

F-15E

The F-15E is a two-seat dual-role fighter capable of performing long-range, deep interdiction missions in all weather, day or night. The aircraft retains its entire air-to-air capability. The prototype was funded internally by McDonnell Douglas and Hughes Aircraft as risk-sharing partners under a project known as "Strike Eagle". The prototype was converted from the second F-15B (71-291) and first flew during August 1981 as part of the Advanced Fighter Capability Demonstrator (AFCD) program.

In production aircraft the rear cockpit has been upgraded with four multi-purpose CRT displays for radar, weapons selection and monitoring of enemy tracking systems and also contains two hand controllers for the radar and LANTIRN/FLIR units. The aft cockpit retains the flight control stick and essential flight instrumentation. A synthetic aperture radar (SAR) feature was added to the AN/APG-70 to provide almost photographic quality imagery in all weather. Front cockpit modifications include redesigned "up-front" controls, a wide field of vision HUD, and three CRTs that provide multi-purpose displays of navigation, weapons delivery, and systems operations, including moving map displays, weapons options, precision radar mapping and terrain following. For tactical target missions at night or in bad weather, the F-15E uses a wide field of vision FLIR (Forward Looking Infrared) and Martin Marietta LANTIRN (Low Altitude Navigation and Targeting Infrared for Night) pods. Successful prototype integration of all these systems was demonstrated during flight tests at Edwards during 1982, and subsequent testing at Eglin.

A digital, triple-redundant Lear Siegler Astronautics flight control system has been installed to permit coupled automatic terrain following. A Honeywell laser gyro inertial navigation system provides quick reaction alignment capabilites.

The 122nd TFS of the Louisiana Air National Guard was the first ANG operator of the F-15A, such as 74-122. Many ANG aircraft have subsequently been modified to include the AN/ALQ-135 ECM system although this aircraft has not.

An F-15A-14-MC (75-0074) of the 555th TFTS/405th TTW shows the black tail codes later adopted by Luke AFB. Note the new style national insignia on fuselage.

The Hawaii ANG (199th TFS/154th CompG) at Hickam AFB operates early F-15A/Bs such as 74-141. "Hawaii" stripe is located on both inside and outside of tails.

Georgia ANG (128th TFS/116th TFW) F-15A, 75-0040 during June of 1986. Unit is based at Dobbins AFB, Georgia. Travel pod with open door is noteworthy.

This F-15A-14-MC (75-0053) was in a "Tiger Meet" and had the outside of its tails painted yellow with black stripes. Aircraft was assigned to the 36th TFW at Bitburg AB.

Some 60% of the F-15's structure was redesigned to create the F-15E, and the airframe is expected to have a 16,000 flight hour fatigue life. To accommodate the new avionics, the forward avionics bays were completely redesigned and the internal fuel capacity was reduced 51 gals. to 2,019 gals. by redesigning the forward fuel tank. The F-15E is the first two-seater to carry AN/ALQ-135 ECM equipment, although to accomplish this the entire 20mm ammunition feed system had to be redesigned and the ammunition capacity cut almost in half. A new common engine bay enables the F-15E to be powered by either the P&W F100-PW-220 or the General Electric F110-GE-100, although all aircraft produced to date have used the Pratt & Whitney engine. This commonality necessitated a complete redesign of the entire aft fuselage. The engine bay structure consists of large titanium sections manufactured with superplastic forming and diffusion bonding processes, and will permit future installation of growth versions of the engines. The F-15E also incorporates digital electronic engine controls, foam filled fuel tanks for greater survivability, higher rated electric generators, an improved environmental control system, strengthened landing gear, and larger wheels and tires.

External identifying features of the F-15E include: bulged main gear doors to accommodate the larger wheel/tire assemblies; a completely redesigned tail hook with no doors; a small bulge on the underside of the fuselage under the 20mm ammunition drum; two AN/ALQ-135B radomes on the aft fuselage booms; and a redesigned fairing between the engine exhaust nozzles.

The AF and McDonnell Douglas began flight testing the new systems for the F-15E on an F-15C (78-0468), F-15B (77-0166) and the prototype Strike Eagle aircraft (71-291) at Edwards during November 1982. 71-291 carried all the production avionics and cockpit displays, but did not include any of the airframe modifications. The aircraft previously had been modified to carry FAST Packs, and had been widely used for early air-to-ground weapons tests. The demonstration program was completed on April 30, 1983 after more than 200 flights. During these tests, 71-921 demonstrated a take-off weight of more than 75,000 lbs. (a 7,000 lb. increase over the F-15C/D). On this occasion the aircraft was equipped with two conformal tanks, three 610 gal. external tanks, and eight 500 lb. Mk 82 bombs. The test program verified 16 different stores configurations, including the carriage of 2,000 lb. Mk 84 bombs and CBU-58 weapons.

After evaluating the potential of the dual-role F-15E against the General Dynamics F-16XL, the AF announced on February 24, 1984 that it had selected the F-15E for continued development. The primary rationale for selecting the F-15E was its lower development costs, projected to be $270 million versus $470 million for the essentially new F-16XL. It also was believed the F-15E had more future growth potential, and was less suscep-

tible to combat damage due to its twin-engine configuration. Design work began during April 1984 under an initial increment of a $359.4 million FPIS contract. The entire development effort and the planned procurement of 392 aircraft was estimated at $1.5 billion FY84 dollars.

Construction of three F-15Es began during July 1985, and the first aircraft made its initial flight on December 11, 1986 piloted by McAir test pilot Gary Jennings. The flight lasted 75 minutes and the aircraft reached 0.9 Mach and 40,000 ft. This aircraft had the redesigned forward fuselage and carried the full complement of F-15E avionics and displays, but did not have the new aft fuselage and common engine bay.

The second and third aircraft generally are considered to be "pre-production" aircraft, with 86-0183 becoming the first to receive the common engine bay ("F110 Compatible Fuselage" officially), and 86-0185 being the first aircraft to incorporate all production F-15E engineering change proposals. Five additional aircraft were ordered during FY86, and the first true production F-15E-42-MC (86-0186), powered by a pair of F100-PW-220 engines, was delivered to the 33rd TFW at Eglin AFB during August 1986 for in-service evaluation.

A total of 42 F-15Es were ordered during FY87, 42 more during FY88 and an additional 36 during FY89. Unfortunately, growing budget pressures have resulted in a concerted effort to cancel further procurement of the F-15E. The AF managed to block attempts to kill the F-15E in the FY90 budget, and an additional 42 aircraft are expected to be ordered during FY90, FY91, and possibly during FY92. Depending exactly when the program is terminated, the AF will be 138-180 aircraft short of their stated goal of 392. The primary rationale for cancelling the program is a report from the Defense Program Analysis and Evaluation Board that states the F-15E will continue to be effective only for the next five years, and that a version of the Navy A-12 Advanced Tactical Aircraft (ATA) is "...the real answer for the mission...", a position not supported by many in the AF.

During May 1989 the AF admitted to problems integrating the AN/ALQ-135B ECM system into production F-15Es. The problems primarily are with revised software written for the F-15E's unique role, and do not effect other AN/ALQ-135 installations in air-superiority configured F-15s. Under Secretary of the AF for Acquisition, John J. Welch, acknowledged that the AN/ALQ-135 "...has been a continuing challenge...", and admitted that the difficulties could delay the 336th TFS's initial operational date into 1990.

Although not frequently discussed, the F-15E may not be the wisest choice for a low-level interdiction platform. Good gust response (how well the aircraft handles up and down drafts) is achieved by a combination of high wing loading and low aspect ratio. The F-15 has an average aspect ratio (around 3), and extremely low (for a modern fighter) wing loading. This combination will probably

make the F-15E a handful for the pilot, and bestow a generally bumpy ride at low levels. Be this as it may, the crews of the F-15E believe that it potentially is one of the outstanding interdiction aircraft of the era.

EXPORT EAGLES

Iran was the first foreign country to take an interest in the F-15 during July 1973 when the Shah personally examined both the F-14 and the F-15 at Andrews AFB, Maryland. Iran needed an aircraft capable of shooting down the MiG-25, and thus chose the Phoenix equipped F-14, since the F-15 had not yet demonstrated this capability. Also, the F-14 was available for earlier delivery than the F-15. As late as 1975, McDonnell Douglas foresaw a possibility of selling 200 F-15s to Germany, 170 to Great Britain, 100 to Japan, 53 to Iran, 50 to Australia, and 50 to Canada. Germany had evaluated the aircraft during March 1975, Canada during June and then again during September 1975, and Great Britain during October 1975. In fact, a sale to France seemed so certain that the second TF-15A (71-291) spent a week painted in French Air Force markings during April 1976 while giving demonstrations to French pilots at Edwards. However, primarily due to its high cost, only three countries, Israel, Japan, and Saudi Arabia, have actually purchased the aircraft to date.

F-15J/DJ

The Japanese Air Self Defense Force (JASDF) conducted two flight evaluations of the F-15 at Edwards during June and July 1975. During early 1977 Japan announced its intentions to purchase a total of 187 single-seat F-15Js and two-seat F-15DJs. These are basically similar to the F-15C/D, minus most of the USAF ECM and nuclear delivery systems. The first 14 aircraft were built by McDonnell Douglas at St. Louis under project Peace Eagle. Two F-15Js (USAF serial numbers 79-0280/0281) were completed by McAir, with the first officially being turned over to the JASDF on July 15, 1980 and the second on July 29. These two F-15Js underwent 39 test flights with JASDF pilots, including weapons firing trials, and subsequently were flown to Japan during March 1981. The remaining 12 U.S.-built aircraft were all two-seat F-15DJs (USAF s/n 79-0282/0287, 81-0068/0071 and 83-0052/0053) with the first of these flying on August 26, 1981, and subsequent delivery on December 11. An additional eight F-15DJs (JASDF serial numbers 22-8803/8810) were shipped to Japan as knocked-down kits for assembly by Mitsubishi.

The first JASDF F-15 Hikotai (squadron) was No. 202 (5th Kokudan [Air Wing]) at Nyutabaru, which was activated during December 1982 with 20 F-15DJs. Other units now equipped are No. 203 (April 1983) and No. 207 (April 1985) Hikotai of the 2nd Kokudan at Chitose, Hokkaido; No. 204 (April 1984, and No. 305 (April 1986) with the 7th Kokudan at Hyakuri; and No. 301 (April 1987) also with the 5th Kokudan at Nyutabaru.

For the 173 aircraft planned to be built in Japan, Mitsubishi is building the forward and center-fuselages, and also is responsible for final assembly and flight testing. Fuji Heavy Industries builds the landing gear doors. Kawasaki is responsible for the wings and tail assemblies, Sumitomo builds the landing gear and IHI builds a version of the F100 engine. Other participants include Shin Meiwa (drop tanks) and Nippi (pylons and missile launchers). The ECM and radar warning system also is of Japanese manufacture. The ECM system, which is generally comparable to the Northrop AN/ALQ-135, is designated J/ALQ-8, while the J/APR-4 radar warning receiver is less sophisticated than the Loral AN/ALR-56. A data link for interfacing with the Japanese GCI (ground control intercept) network also is fitted. A total of 136 aircraft had been funded through FY86, and approximately 126 had been delivered by the spring of 1989.

ISRAEL

Four Israeli pilots and one radar operator flew the first TF-15A (71-290) at Edwards during September 1974. This was Israel's first formal evaluation of the F-15, and the aircraft was pitted against a slatted F-4E during air combat maneuvers. Israel's *Heyl Ha' Avir* since has received four Category II test F-15As (72-116/118 and 72-120) refurbished under the *Peace Fox I* program and delivered on December 10, 1976. Israel subsequently purchased an additional 19 F-15As (76-1505/1523), and two F-15Bs (76-1524/1525) under *Peace Fox II*, and 18 F-15Cs (80-0122/0130 and 83-0054/0062) and 8 F-15Ds (80-0131/0136 and 83-0063/0064) under *Peace Fox III*. Israel is the only foreign country to operate the F-15A/B models. The Israeli aircraft differ from the U.S. F-15s in having AN/ARC-109 radios in place of the AN/ARC-164 unit, and the nuclear delivery systems have been deleted. Israeli aircraft are capable of carrying an indigenously produced AL/L-8202 ECM pod in addition to U.S. supplied AN/ALQ-119(V) and AN/ALQ-131 pods. All Israeli aircraft use the IC-7 ejection system instead of the ACES II used by later U.S. F-15C/Ds. All *Heyl Ha' Avir* F-15s, including the four refurbished test aircraft, are capable of carrying conformal fuel tanks, which are manufactured locally by Israeli Aircraft Industries (IAI). The Israeli F-15s also were the first to be equipped with chaff/flare dispensing units. Israel purchased additional *Eagles* (seven F-15Cs and four F-15Ds) during early 1989 for use as long-range strike aircraft. Although no details have been released, it is believed that these aircraft will utilize the basic airframe from the F-15E since McAir no longer is producing the original F-15C/D airframe. They undoubtedly will have conventional F-15C/D cockpits and avionics.

The Israeli *Eagles* first went into battle on June 27, 1979 when they downed four Syrian MiG-21s in air com-

bat above Lebanon. On June 7, 1981 the F-15s flew top cover for a strike force in a raid on the Osirak nuclear reactor near Baghdad, Iraq. During the 1982 Israeli invasion of Lebanon, the F-15s are believed to have shot down at least three high-flying MiG-25 *Foxbats* using AIM-7s and "zoom-climb" (also called "snap-up") intercepts. To date, the Israeli F-15s are believed to have shot down 62 fixed wing aircraft and one helicopter. Two *Heyl Ha' Avir* squadrons, Nos. 133 and 106 fly the F-15.

KINGDOM OF SAUDI ARABIA

The Royal Saudi Air Force obtained 46 F-15Cs (80-0062/0106 and 81-0002) and 16 F-15Ds (80-0107/0121 and 81-0003) under project *Peace Sun* to replace their aging BAC *Lightnings*, with the first F-15D arriving in Saudi Arabia on August 11, 1981. The original Saudi order was for 47 F-15Cs and 15 F-15Ds, but on the production line a USAF F-15D (81-0066) was swapped for an RSAF F-15C (81-0003) which became USAF F-15C 81-0056, with the new Saudi two-seater carrying the same serial number as the single-seater it replaced (81-0003). Apparently the Camp David accords specified that no more than 60 *Eagles* would be in Saudi Arabia at one time, and consequently the last two aircraft initially were retained at McAir in St. Louis as attrition aircraft. At least one Saudi aircraft has been lost due to a landing accident. Three Saudi squadrons, No. 13 at Dhahran, No. 6 at Taif, and an unidentified squadron at Khamis Mushayt currently fly the F-15. On June 5, 1984 two Iranian F-4 *Phantom IIs* were shot down over the Persian Gulf by Saudi F-15s after receiving intercept instructions from an orbiting E-3A AWACS. Saudi aircraft are capable of being equipped with conformal fuel tanks, although it is unclear if any CFTs actually were delivered to the RSAF due to political considerations.

In a move to ensure the continued availability of attrition aircraft, Saudi Arabia ordered an additional 12 F-15C/Ds during early 1989. As with the latest Israeli order, it is likely that these aircraft will use the basic F-15E airframe since the original F-15C/D no longer is in production. These aircraft will be stored at the McAir facility in St. Louis, and dispatched to Saudi Arabia as needed. The Defense Department notified Congress during June 1989 of its intent to sell Saudi Arabia modification kits valued at $350 million for the P&W F100-PW-100 engines in the RSAF F-15s. The kits convert the engines to the newer F100-PW-220 configuration. The twelve new aircraft purchased earlier in 1989 will be delivered with the upgraded engines.

TESTBEDS

During May 1971 McAir received a contract to develop a composite wing for the F-15 consisting of boron and graphite filaments embedded in epoxy resin. The wing

was to be 500 lbs. lighter with a longer fatigue life than the metal wing used in production aircraft. Structural test articles were completed and flight tests were scheduled for late-1975. Unfortunately the project was cancelled during February 1975, but the technology later was used in the F/A-18A and AV-8B projects. A subsequent project did result in the first F-15B (71-290) flying with aluminum-lithium (Al-Li) wing panels which were 5% stronger and 9% lighter than the conventional aluminum panels they replaced. Flight tests started during the summer of 1986, and are continuing aboard 71-290 in its role as the F-15S/MTD demonstrator. Although never adopted for production on the F-15, these tests did prove the worth of this new lightweight metal for use on high performance aircraft.

During 1974 McAir received a $6 million contract from the AF Flight Dynamics Laboratory at Wright-Patterson AFB, Ohio, to design and built an advanced environmental control system (AECS) for use in the F-15. The AF had evaluated aircraft electronic system failures and found that 52% of them were related directly to temperature, humidity, or dust. Chief engineer for McAir was Virgil M. Marti, who led a team to develop a high-capacity cooling system, complete with dust separators and a dehumidifier. In addition to maintaining lower temperatures in the electronics, the system reduced windscreen fog, and provided a more comfortable cockpit, since the cockpit shared the same environmental unit. The system was flight tested aboard an F-15A-2-MC (71-282) at Edwards during the spring of 1978, and at NAS Dallas during September 1978.

During February 1982 McAir was awarded a 15-month contract by the Flight Dynamics Laboratory (FDL) to demonstrate an advanced integrated flight control/fire control system under the "Integrated Flight Fire-Control (IFFC)" program, also known as "Firefly III". The program involved extensive simulation at the FDL and McAir, and then flight tests in a modified F-15A at both Edwards and Nellis. The IFFC allows a sensor locked on a target to effectively fly the aircraft to weapons release or gun-firing position. Development flights began during April 1982 on F-15B-20-MC (77-0166) equipped with IFFC and an Automatic Tracking Laser Illumination System (ALTIS II) pod on the forward port-side AIM-7 station. During these trials, air-to-air weapons were fired at simulated targets while the F-15 was maneuvered at high offset angles, demonstrating its ability to employ weapons accurately while in three-dimensional flight. This allowed the F-15 an earlier opportunity to fire, and also extended the time available for firing during a dogfight.

Another attempt at decreasing the structural weight of the aircraft was made on October 11, 1985 when McAir received a contract from ASD for the construction of two composite horizontal stabilators. The program started during February 1986 and was completed during

A 325th TTW F-15B-13-MC (75-0082) from Tyndall AFB with an inert AIM-7 "Sparrow" and AIM-9 "Sidewinder". Note lack of AN/ALQ-128 radome on rear of left fin-tip pod.

Note new-style national insignia on this F-15A-15-MC (76-0024) from the Massachusetts ANG's 101st FIS/102nd FIW. Extensive markings on external tanks are noteworthy.

An F-15A-16-MC (76-0059) from the 1st TFW lands during the first deployment of a stateside "Eagle" unit to Europe. Aircraft carried three 610 gal. external tanks.

An F-15A-16-MC (76-0080) assigned to the 318th FIS sits on the ramp at Castle AFB, California during May 1984. ADTAC units initially displayed colorful tail markings.

September 1986. Two complete horizontal stabilators were produced, with one being used for static tests and the other undergoing ground vibration tests after installation in an F-15B (71-290). Each torque box consisted of a substructure made of superplastically-formed and diffusion bonded titanium with the skins consisting of boron fiber composite coated with boron carbide. The coating allowed the fiber to retain strength during the manufacture process. The leading and trailing edges were made of superplastically-formed aluminum to avoid corrosion. The project demonstrated a 50% cost reduction over the current machined titanium substructure, and also yielded a 17% weight reduction. Many of the techniques learned were subsequently applied to the F-15E.

F-15S/MTD (NF-15B)

During October 1984 McDonnell Douglas was awarded a $117.8 million cost-sharing contract to develop and flight test an advanced technology version of the F-15. The contract has an eventual value of $272 million, with industry contributing slightly less than half the costs. The industry team includes prime contractor McDonnell Douglas and major subcontractors Pratt & Whitney (engines and nozzles), General Electric (flight control computer and software implementation), Cleveland Pneumatic (landing gear), and National Water Lift (hydraulic actuators). Program manager for McAir is Ken Token, while Lt.Col. Felix Sanchez fills the role for the AF.

This aircraft, commonly called the F-15S/MTD (STOL/Maneuvering Technology Demonstrator), is to investigate four specific technologies: two-dimensional (2-D) thrust vectoring/reversing jet nozzles; integrated flight/propulsion controls; rough/soft field landing gear; and advanced vehicle/pilot interfaces. It is intended primarily as a flight test vehicle for emerging technologies that have potential application to the AF Advanced Tactical Fighter (YF-22/YF-23). The aircraft was largely patterned after a concept proposed by McAir for the AFTI demonstrator program that eventually was awarded to General Dynamics using a modified F-16.

McDonnell Douglas has modified the first F-15B (71-290) for the flight test program, with the aircraft being redesignated NF-15B. Changes include controllable foreplanes, modified from F/A-18A *Hornet* tailplanes, mounted above the engine inlet trunks forward of the wings. The foreplanes are mounted at a dihedral angle of 20%, and can operate symmetrically or asymmetrically to provide pitch and roll moments, and are used as stability maintaining surfaces instead of for primary flight control. In theory they permit the F-15B's maximum allowable load factor to be increased above 9.0 g without additional structural reinforcement. The aircraft also is fitted with F-15E style rough/soft-field landing gear and a cockpit basically similar to the F-15E. Provisions for an AN/APG-70 radar unit with synthetic aperture features, and LANTRIN navigation pods also have been incorporated into the aircraft. The actual installation of this equipment will necessitate the removal of the test boom currently fitted to the aircraft's nose, and will be accomplished late in the test program.

Rectangular, two-dimensional vectoring nozzles manufactured from titanium and carbon-fiber are installed at the rear of modified F100-PW-220 engines, replacing the F-15's standard afterburner ducts. The nozzles can vector engine thrust ±20° from the longitudinal axis to enhance take-off performance and maneuverability, and also are designed to provide any level of reverse thrust throughout the flight envelope, including approach and landing. It is expected that full application of reverse thrust will reduce the F-15S/MTD's landing roll to about 28% of the distance required by a conventional F-15. The primary propulsion system modifications include the addition of a nozzle controller that communicates with the engine's standard DEEC, and changes to the engine's fan ducts. The ducts were modified to withstand the pitch vectoring loads that develop when the 2-D nozzles are vectored. Four 2-D engine/nozzle units have been constructed by P&W; two for ground tests, which will total about 350 hrs., and two for flight tests. The 2-D nozzle provides an exhaust area roughly equivalent to that of a standard F100-PW-220 axisymmetric nozzle. The engine/nozzle can be vectored from +20° to −20° in approximately 0.5 seconds, and can go from full afterburner to full reverse thrust in about 1.5 seconds. The modified powerplants are said to be "...slightly heavier..." than standard F100-PW-220s.

Initial test flights with the new foreplanes and conventional axisymmetric exhaust nozzles began on September 7, 1988 and continued until January 1989. These flights originally were scheduled to include the 2-D nozzles, but development problems delayed the delivery of some components until early 1989. During these flights the aircraft reached a maximum altitude of 48,000 ft. and a speed of 1.7 Mach during 41 hrs. accumulated in 43 flights. The two-dimensional nozzles were fitted to the aircraft during spring 1989, and McAir pilot Larry Walker took the modified aircraft for its first flight on May 10, 1989. During this flight the aircraft reached 20,000 ft. and 0.9 Mach and the aircraft's exhaust nozzles were used in a conventional mode, with thrust vectoring and reversing not attempted. An additional four flights conducted from the Lambert-St. Louis International Airport verified the ability of the aircraft to fly to Edwards. A speed of 1.85 Mach at 48,000 ft. was reached during these flights. The aircraft was ferried to Edwards on June 16 for a flight test program that will run through January 1990. The aircraft is expected to fly 60 test missions at a nominal rate of two per week, although this may change once the aircraft is cleared for aerial refueling.

Early ground tests of the engine/nozzle have revealed several small problems, including a convergent flap liner that limited the use of afterburner to a few seconds. A bearing in the nozzle's thrust reverser mechanism also failed. A new flap liner has been developed and successfully tested, but a revised bearing is proving to be more of a challenge. Initial tests of a redesigned bearing currently are scheduled for late-July 1989. The propulsion units are being tested at the Pratt & Whitney facility in West Palm Beach, Florida, as well as undergoing altitude testing at the NASA Lewis Research Center in Ohio. Installing the new bearing in the flight nozzles at Edwards could take six to eight weeks, effectively halting the program for that length of time.

A four channel digital FBW system integrates with the flight control system and controls all functions of the foreplanes, ailerons, horizontal tail surfaces, and vectoring nozzles to provide high precision control of the aircraft. A key capability of this new system to be demonstrated during the flight test series is called "autoguidance" which allows accurate landings without the use of ground navigational aids. During these tests, the pilot will identify a distant landing strip using the AN/APG-70 SAR and LANTRIN, and designate a landing point using a high-resolution ground map displayed on a cockpit CRT. Aircraft systems will provide the pilot with azimuth and elevation steering commands on the HUD. The commands will allow the pilot to fly a glideslope for touchdown on the previously designated landing point. The F-15S/MTD incorporates wing panels of new aluminum-lithium (Al-Li) alloys that are 5% stronger and 9% lighter than the conventional aluminum parts they replace. Flight tests of the new pieces began aboard 71-290 during the summer of 1986, before its F-15S/MTD conversion.

Performance parameters specified for the F-15S/MTD include take-off and landing runs of 1,500 ft. on a 50 ft. wide hard, wet, rough surface runway at night and in adverse weather, with full internal fuel and 6,000 lbs. of ordnance. McDonnell Douglas has stated that it is predicting a take-off run of 1,000 ft. and a landing run of 1,250 ft. on wet runways with crosswinds up to 30 knots. A 10,000 lb. increase in payload when operating from a 1,500 ft. runway also is anticipated. Air combat maneuvering will be enhanced by a 53% improvement in roll rate with up to a 33% improvement in pitch rate. The additional weight and drag of the modifications are expected to decrease the cruising radius by 4%. A total of ten test flights have been allocated to develop and demonstrate in-flight thrust vectoring/reversal in combat situations. Other benefits to future programs from two-dimensional exhaust nozzles include smaller vertical fins (since the nozzles can provide some ptich and yaw control), and eliminating the need for a speed brake.

NASA

Two of the Category I development F-15As (71-281 and 71-287) were acquired by NASA's Dryden Flight Research Center for a variety of test projects. During early 1980 71-281 was used to flight test tiles for the Space Shuttle orbiter. The tiles were subjected to approximately one and one-half times the dynamic pressure the shuttle undergoes during ascent. Tiles mounted on the right wing of the F-15 siumlated the leading edge of the orbiter's wing, while tiles on the left wing represented tiles on the junction of the orbiter's wing and fuselage. The tests observed the effects of the dynamic pressure on various adhesives and water repellant compounds. 71-281 was retired from service during 1983, and placed on display at Langley AFB, Virginia. 71-287 currently sports an all-white paint scheme, and continues to be flown at Dryden with the Ames NASA number 835.

During 1982 and early-1983 NASA tested a digital electronic engine control (DEEC) advanced fuel management system in support of the F100-PW-220 development aboard 71-287. The system was based on a 16-bit microprocessor with 8.5k of memory which controlled the gas generator and afterburner control units. During the summer of 1983, 71-287 was used in a further series of demonstrations for the Engine Model Derivative (EMD, now called the Improved Performance Engine—IPE). These tests demonstrated that relatively modest engine improvements could drastically improve performance: acceleration from 0.8 Mach to 2.0 Mach was improved 41% at 35,000 ft., as well as improved air-start capabilities and better specific fuel consumption figures.

During May 1989, special equipment aboard 71-287 correctly identified and isolated a simulated flight control system failure while in flight. NASA project manager Dr. James Stewart considered this test to be a breakthrough in computer-based diagnostics. This is one of several technologies to be investigated during the joint NASA/AF Self-Repairing Flight Control Program scheduled to begin during the fall of 1989. Other elements of this project include failure detection and identification, followed by automatic reconfiguration of the flight control system. This would involve the system automatically reconfiguring itself to redistribute a failed (or missing) flight control surface's functions to the other flight control surfaces, a much more advanced version of a rudimentary capability the F-15 already has. As currently conceived, the system would alert the pilot, identify the problem, display the revised aircraft configuration, and define a new allowable flight envelope. The two main contractors involved in the program are McAir and the General Electric Aircraft Control Systems Division of Binghamton, New York.

PROPOSALS AND OTHER DREAMS

The first derivative study of the F-15 was an interceptor working in conjunction with the Airborne Warning and Control System (AWACS) E-3A during 1971-72. The AF instituted a series of studies (Advanced Manned Interceptor, CONUS Interceptor, etc.) for a new interceptor and had considered a wide variety of possibilities, including a modified Lockheed YF-12A, an improved General Dynamics F-106, and the Grumman F-14. The YF-12 and F-106 were dropped from consideration during late-1971, and the F-14 generally was rated at par or slightly better than the F-15 in the interceptor role. The studies also included a stretched, F100 powered F-111, designated F-111X-7, and a modified North American RA-5C powered by three J79s and designated NR-349. Initial funding consisted of $5 million during FY73 money for continued engineering studies, but the program was canceled shortly thereafter, the existing ADC F-106s continuing to serve until they were replaced by F-15As beginning during the early-1980s.

Another variant that has been proposed since the beginning of the F-15 project is the RF-15 reconnaissance aircraft. There have been several variations to this theme, one involving a special nose with camera ports, similar in concept to that employed on the RF-4B/C. This version also employed a TV camera, multi-spectral scanner and side-looking radar in a modified lower fuselage. However, generally the modifications are limited to data processing equipment, with all sensor equipment to be contained in FAST Packs. The AF has never enthusiastically supported the idea of an RF-15, mainly because of its potential cost. As a private venture McDonnell Douglas also has developed a conformal reconnaissance pod designed to be carried instead of the centerline stores station of two-seat F-15s under the internal F-15(R) *"Peep Eagle"* program. The pod began flight tests during the summer of 1987 aboard 71-291. The Reconnaissance Technology Demonstrator (RTD) pod can carry a full range of current AF camera and imaging equipment. Optionally, it is capable of transmitting imagery data to ground stations directly. Special conformal fuel tanks could provide additional volume for equipment. This might finally make the concept of an RF-15 a reality, and there has been considerable interest from some of the F-15's foreign customers.

McDonnell Douglas has periodically proposed a version of the two-seat F-15 as the heir-apparent to the F-4G Advanced *Wild Weasel* defense suppression aircraft. The McAir demonstrator F-15B (71-291) was flight tested with an aerodynamic pod under its nose, vaguely reminiscent of the F-4G chin pod, that was intended to hold the AN/APR-38 *Wild Weasel* system. While generally endorsed by the AF, the expense of the aircraft makes its

Two F-15As (including 76-0086) were modified to carry the Vought Anti-Satellite (ASAT) missile on their centerline pylons. Note satellite-killer insignia on vertical stabilizer.

This F-15A-17-MC (76-0097) is assigned to the 49th TFW at Holloman AFB. Checkerboards around top of vertical stabilizers are red and white.

The older F-15As (such as 76-0126) have been assigned to various fighter interceptor squadrons, such as the 48th FIS. Tail markings are light blue and white.

The newest F-15 squadron is the 123rd FIS/142nd FIG of the Oregon ANG which received its first aircraft during August 1989. 76-0139 is an F-15B-17-MC.

The 4485th TS at Eglin continues to perform operational testing, hence the "OT" tailcode on this F-15A-18-MC (77-0064). The tails have black and white checkerboards.

An F-15A-18-MC (77-0074) assigned to the 32nd TFS at Soesterberg AB, Netherlands, touches down. The squadron's tail stripe is dark orange.

The Warner-Robins ALC originally used the WR tailcode on its F-15A-18-MC (77-0068). Red, white, and blue stripes on tail and eagle motif on nose are noteworthy.

WRALC has since changed to a somewhat less colorful paint scheme with RG tailcode. ALC badge is visible on tail.

This very clean looking 49th TFW F-15A-19-MC (77-0119) passed through Offutt AFB during June 1984. No wing pylons appear to be fitted to the aircraft.

The 48th FIS traded its colorful ADTAC markings for standard-looking LY tailcodes. Placement of nose markings varies from squadron to squadron.

The 3247th TS/3246th TW uses AD tailcodes to symbolize "Armament Division", even though they are now called "Munitions Division". Placement of tail stripe is somewhat lower than the usual operational squadron location.

F-15B-20-MC (77-0166) participated in the IFFC/"Firefly III" program. Note the Automatic Tracking Laser Illumination System (ALTIS) pod on the forward port-side AIM-7 station and the modifications to the AIM-7 attach point.

adaption for this role seem unlikely. Nevertheless, during May 1986, McAir received a $500,000, 10-month, study contract for continued development under the "Wild Weasel 7" nomenclature. If approved, the anticipated service date of the new *Wild Weasel* aircraft is 1997-98, and they would be converted from existing F-15B/D airframes.

F-15(N) AND F-15(N-PHX)

McAir spent considerable time and effort from 1970 to 1974 to define several versions of the F-15 for naval service. An unofficial (and perhaps, unwelcome) title of "Seagle" was applied by various organizations involved. The first presentation to the Navy occurred during July 1971. McAir's position was that due to its excellent thrust-to-weight ratio and good visibility, the F-15 could easily be adapted for carrier operations. The only modifications required to enable it to operate off of CVA-19 class (or larger) carriers were: strengthened landing gear; an extendable front landing gear strut to produce the proper angle of attack upon catapult launch; installation of a nose-tow catapult system; folding wings; and a beefed-up arresting hook and associated structure. Both the nose and main landing gear wells would have to be enlarged to accommodate the increased stroke of the new gear. These modifications would add approximately 2,300 lbs. to the basic F-15A.

The Navy was not overly impressed with this proposal, so McAir further modified the design. Two McAir models (199A-11A and 199A-12) then were presented to the Navy. Model 199A-12 featured a bridle catapult attachment, while 199A-11A had a nose-tow catapult attachment, otherwise they were identical. The design also featured a dual nose wheel arrangement, increased fuselage structural strength, a Navy-type refueling probe, and most important, an improved high-lift system, in addition to all the originally proposed modifications. The high-lift system was composed of full-span leading edge flaps, BLC trailing edge flaps and a slotted aileron, all of which contributed 632 lbs. to the projected 3,055 lb. increase (to 42,824 lbs.) over the AF F-15A. An additional 71.9 lbs. would be added for Navy avionics, including: AN/ASN-54(V) approach power compensator set; AN/ASW-27B digital data communications set; AN/ALQ-100

deceptive countermeasures set; AN/ALQ-91A countermeasures set; AN/APN-15(V) radar beacon set; AN/ARA-63 receiver decoding group and an AN/APN-194 radar altimeter. The USAF-standard TEWS ECM system would be deleted.

These versions of the F-15(N) still were armed the same as the AF F-15A (M61A1, AIM-7, and AIM-9), and were deemed roughly equal to the F-14B in overall performance, except for range. The radius of action in a fighter-escort configuration was 271 nm on internal fuel, compared to 481 nm for the F-14B and 319 for the F-4J. With external tanks, this increased to 516 nm versus 685 for the F-14B and 485 for the F-4J. No data was generated for FAST Pack equipped aircraft. A total of $403.5 million was projected for non-recurring engineering costs, with a flyaway price of $7.6 million based on a 313 aircraft production run.

The F-15N then became the subject of Navy Fighter Study Group III. This group disregarded the McAir data, enlarged the nose to carry the AN/AWG-9 radar, and added *Phoenix* missiles resulting in an aircraft that weighed 10,000 lbs. more than the basic F-15A. This weight increase, along with the associated drag, greatly decreased the performance of the F-15, negating any advantage it had over the F-14A. There also was considerable concern over the 12° angle-of-attack used by the F-15 (compared to 10.2° for the F-14A) during approaches, and the relatively narrow-track of its landing gear.

McAir and Hughes countered the study group's criticisms with a further modified version known as F-15(N-PHX), which added a rudimentary AIM-54 *Phoenix* missile capability. This version (model 199A-19B) took the model 199A-11A and modified the AN/APG-63 radar set into an AN/APG-64. These modifications involved increasing the transmit power to 7 kW (compared to 10kW in the AN/AWG-9 and 5.2 kW in the AN/APG-63), a command link, a track-while-scan capability, and a missile test feature. The radar antenna also was modified to effect a slight frequency shift. The central computer had its load changed to support the new track-while-scan modes, as well as adding additional memory and *Phoenix* unique software. Some cockpit controls and displays also were modified. The aircraft could carry up to eight

AIM-54s: one on each fuselage AIM-7 station, one on each inboard wing pylon, and two (in tandem) on a special centerline pylon. The appropriate missile cooling systems were added to each station. Take-off gross weight was up to 46,009 lbs. The high-lift devices were changed to include full-span Krueger leading edge flaps, BLC trailing edge flaps, and single-slotted ailerons. Approach speed to a carrier was estimated at 136 knots.

Another proposal also was presented, one essentially echoing the results of Navy Fighter Study Group III. The aircraft was equipped with the Hughes AN/AWG-9 weapons control group from the F-14A, but otherwise resembled the earlier F-15(N-PHX). Estimated non-recurring R&D costs were $1.173 billion in FY72 dollars. Based on a 313 unit production run, the flyaway cost was $11.5 million per aircraft.

On March 30, 1973, the Senate Armed Services Committee's ad hoc Tactical Air Power subcommittee started new discussions on the possibilities of modifying the F-15 for the Navy mission. At this point the F-14 program was having difficulties, and the subcommittee wanted to look at possible alternatives, namely lower-cost (stripped) F-14s, F-15Ns, and improved F-4s. There were even proposals by Senator Eagleton for a "fly-off" between the F-14 and F-15, but this never transpired. These discussions, along with some other considerations, led to the forming of Navy Fighter Study Group IV, out of which the aircraft ultimately known as F/A-18A was born.

OPERATIONAL SERVICE:

The first operational aircrft, TF-15A-7-MC 73-108 ("TAC-1") was accepted formally during ceremonies at Luke AFB, Arizona, on November 14, 1974 and was assigned to the 555th TFTS, 58th TFTW. President Gerald R. Ford presided over the ceremonies watched by some 22,000 spectators. Two additional 58th squadrons, the 461st and 550th, received F-15s, and all were used to train pilots, flight instructors, and ground crews. The 58th TFTW was redesignated as the 58th TTW, which operates four squadrons (the original three, plus the 426th TFTS) of various model F-15s, including the F-15E. This Wing provides initial training to all U.S., Saudi, and Israeli pilots, and trained the cadre of Japanese instructors.

As part of an operational readiness test during 1976, an F-15 from Luke intercepted a Boeing IM-99 *Bomarc* target missile flying at 68,000 ft. and a speed of Mach 2.7, and destroyed the drone with an AIM-7F *Sparrow III*. Although this success was reported widely in the press, this test and others showed the *Sparrow* still has considerable difficulty intercepting maneuvering targets, or targets located in ground clutter.

During 1976, the second TF-15A (71-291) conducted a world tour to celebrate the American Bicentennial and to promote the F-15 overseas. Painted in a bicentennial red, white, and blue paint scheme, this aircraft logged over 34,000 miles during a two and one-half month period while also logging more than 100 flight hours and averaging more than one flight per day. In the course of this journey, it became the first fighter to fly non-refueled across the Australian continent. The trip also included stops in Alconbury, England; Bitburg, Germany; Yokota, Japan; Osan and Kunsan, Korea; Kadena, Okinawa; Clark AB in the Philippines; Guam; Hawaii; and Luke AFB.

The first operational wing to receive the *Eagle* was the 1st TFW at Langley AFB, Virginia, beginning on January 9, 1976, with the first aircraft (74-0083) named "*Peninsula Patriot*". The three squadrons within the Wing now are assigned to the Rapid Deployment Force, and fly F-15C/Ds. About the same time as the 1st TFW was getting their aircraft, problems began to surface at Luke. The F-15 had been fielded with an advertised capability of 1.13 sorties per day, but in real-life was averaging about 0.61. There were several factors involved in this failing, primarily that the mean-time-between-failures (MTBF) was less than half of what had been predicted. It took longer to diagnose problems than originally thought, and there was a lack of spare parts in the logistics system to repair the failures once found. The engines placed the largest demands on the maintenance effort, with about 15 maintenance man-hours per flight hour (MMH/FH)[2], or almost half of the 31 MMH/FH required for the entire aircraft. This was over twice the powerplant maintenance (per engine) required on the F-16A, which uses the same engine. The complex fire-control system also was producing its share of headaches, although these were eased as more capable automated diagnostic equipment was fielded and the avionics configuration stabilized.

By January 1977, 143 aircraft had been delivered, these accumulating 25,031 flight hours during 19,626 flights. Fifty-one aircraft were at Luke (58th TFTW), 63 at Langley (1st TFW), and 2 at Nellis (57th FWW). The St. Louis factory was producing new aircraft at the rate of nine per month. The F-15 was introduced to Europe with a mass deployment during June 1977 when twenty-three *Eagles* from the 36th TFW departed Langley and flew 3,600 miles in seven and one-half hours to Bitburg, Germany. Led by Gen. Fred C. Kyler, commander of the 36th, the F-15s cruised at 38,000 ft. and 500 mph, refueling several times from KC-135 tankers enroute.

During March 1977, the commander of AFSC, Gen. Alton D. Slay, spent several days in front of the Senate Armed Services Committee explaining the reasons for the dismal F-15 readiness rates, most of which centered around engine problems. During April 1977, the AF raised the allowable operating time for the P&W F100 from 500 to 750 hrs. after several engines in the *"Pacer Century"* program successfully passed the 500 hr. mark with no problems revealed during tear-down inspections. *"Pacer Century"* was a program conducted in which 12 production engines were flown at accelerated rates to gain reliability and maintainability data. The program involved six engines with the 58th TFTW at Luke and six engines with the 1st TFW at Langley. With the engine problems at least partially cured, the readiness rates for the F-15 climbed back to an acceptable level, and would increase further as the new electronic systems became more reliable.

The 57th Fighter Weapons Wing (FWW) at Nellis AFB also received 14 *Eagles* during 1977, with all of them being assigned to the 433rd FWS. The 57th's job was to continue FOT&E and also develop tactics for F-15 use.

As of September 30, 1977, 245 *Eagles* had been delivered, flying 58,800 hrs. in 43,900 flights. The 58th TTW had 50 aircraft, the 1st TFW had 76, the 57th FWW had 14, and the 36th TFW at Bitburg was up to full strength with 73 aircraft. Also during 1977, the 57th FWW's F-15s participated in a test program called AIMVAL/ACEVAL (Air Intercept Missile Evaluation/Air Combat Evaluation). This was a joint AF/Navy program to evaluate current and future air-to-air missiles on the air combat maneuvering range located at Nellis. The tests also evaluated the impact of differing numbers of combatants on each side during air-to-air combat. The program lasted approximately 10 months and involved F-15s and F-14s on the Blue force, versus F-5E and T-38s on the Red force.

During 1977 the 49th TFW at Holloman AFB, New Mexico transitioned into the F-15A/B from F-4s, with the last being released on December 20, 1977. On September 13, 1978, Operation *Coronet Sandpiper* brought the first F-15A to the 32nd TFS at Camp New Amsterdam (Soesterberg) AB in the Netherlands. The aircraft were accepted officially by Lt.Gen. Benjamin N. Nellis, who had left the F-15 SPO to become USAFE Vice Commander. The 33rd TFW at Eglin AFB began to receive F-15A/Bs on December 15, 1978. During January 1979, 12 F-15s from the 1st TFW at Langley deployed with E-3A AWACS aircraft to Saudi Arabia, which had just purchased both E-3s and F-15s.

Engine problems continued to plague the F-15, with afterburner failures and engine stagnation being factors in five of the nine crashes as of April 1979. AF and industry teams modified the aircraft's jet fuel starter to facilitate in-flight restarts, restricted afterburner use, and modified engine maintenance procedures. In trying to find a common cause for five engine related accidents by the 36th TFW alone, afterburner hard-starts were blamed for more than three-quarters of all F100 stagnation stalls. During a November 1979 report, Gen. Slay described 755 stall stagnations in 1,385 operational engines.[3]

---

[2] Maintenance man hours per flight hour is the measure of how much maintenance it takes to keep an aircraft flying. The P-51 during 1944 averaged about 8 MMH/FH, while the F-5A during 1965 averaged about 16. The highest recorded to date for an operational weapons system is 52 MMH/FH for the early F-111D. The F-15's designers spent considerable effort in designing the F-15 to be easily maintained, with an estimate of between 8 and 10 MMH/FH. By the time the Category II testing was complete, the figure was down to 19, but engine problems forced this number back up to about 32 during 1979.

[3] It is interesting to note that P&W identified three modifications to the F100-PW-100 engine, but due to budgetary restrictions only two were incorporated into engines destined for the F-15. The third was approved only for F-16 engines with the rationale being the F-15 has two engines, and hence an extra margin of safety.

In spite of these problems, by the end of 1979 the F-15's loss rate was less than half that of any other fighter in AF history at the same point operationally. 1978 and 1979 were the first years that the F-15s were deployed globally, with F-15s based at 10 locations in four countries deploying to 12 other countries: Greece; the UK; Spain; Denmark; Pakistan; Norway; Belgium; Italy; Korea; Japan; the Philippines; and Canada.

The first unit to receive F-15C/Ds was the 18th TFW at Kadena, Okinawa, during September 1979. Almost all the original F-15A squadrons later traded their early models for F-15C/Ds. The F-15As were transferred to four Air Defense TAC squadrons (the 5th, 48th, 57th, and 318th FIS), and various Air National Guard units. Two test squadrons, two at Eglin (448th TS and 3246th TW/TAWC) and one at Edwards (6512 TS) also flew (and continue to fly) various F-15 models.

Fortunately, the introductin of the improved electronics on the F-15C, as well as the continued improvement in the F-15A's systems, has increased the operational readiness rate to an acceptable level. The introduction of the F100-PW-220 engine, with its electronic engine controls, has greatly reduced the number and frequency of stall/stagnations, and also has dropped the MMH/FH for the F-15 (down to around 14) to the second lowest for any operational fighter (the F-16, by virtue of its single engine, is averaging about 10 MMH/FH). Additionally, the increased engine reliability has further lowered the F-15 loss rate, and at one million flight hours it is the safest fighter in the history of the AF.

The 336th FTS of the 4th TFW at Seymour-Johnson AFB, South Carolina, became the first operational squadron to receive F-15E dual-role fighters. Their first aircraft arrived on December 29, 1988, and by April 1989,

four more had been accepted. The squadron is expected to become operational during October 1989, but problems with integrating the F-15E's dedicated AN/ALQ-135B may delay that. A second squadron, probably the 334th TFS, is due to receive their first F-15E during mid-1989.

PROJECT *STREAK EAGLE*

For two weeks beginning on January 16, 1975, three AF pilots and a modified F-15A-6-MC (72-119) made an assault on the world class time-to-climb for aircraft powered by jet engines. The three pilots, Maj. Roger Smith, Maj. W. R. ''Mac'' Macfarlane, and Maj. Dave Peterson all were members of the F-15 Joint Test Force at Edwards. Pete Garrison, a McAir pilot, was instrumental in the development of the flight profiles used for the records. Project *Streak Eagle* had three major objectives:

- To enhance AF esprit de corps and morale, and to foster the attractiveness of an AF career in support of recruiting objectives,
- To help establish the credibility of AF general purpose forces as an integral element of the United States' overall military posture,
- To provide data on the F-15's capabilities at the extremes of altitudes and performance under controlled test conditions.

The AF awarded McAir a $2.1 million dollar contract on April 1, 1974 for aircraft modifications and general support, with configuration approval on May 18, 1974. All test aircraft then in inventory were evaluated, and the choice narrowed between F5 (71-284) and F17 (72-119). Several items led to the choice of 72-119: it was 800 lbs. lighter than F5; it was an AF (Cat II) aircraft as opposed to a con-

The first F-15C (78-0468) is shown with the type-4 CFTs destined for the F-15E. These CFTs are equipped for ''tangential carriage'' of weapons on stub pylons instead of MERs which greatly reduces parasitic drag.

The first operational F-15C (78-0469), and another F-15C-21-MC (78-0491) assigned to the 18th TFW at Kadena AB, Okinawa are each carrying three 610 gal. drop tanks. Note lack of squadron identifying stripe on tail.

F-15C-23-MC (78-0542) is assigned to the 4485th TestS at Eglin. At right it displays the 1982-style OT&E tailcodes, while at left the more ''official'' OT tailcodes of 1988 are shown. Note change in position of some markings on nose and squadron patch on air intake trunk. Purpose of dark patch ahead of refueling receptacle in left photo is unknown.

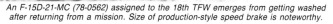

An F-15D-21-MC (78-0562) assigned to the 18th TFW emerges from getting washed after returning from a mission. Size of production-style speed brake is noteworthy.

Fully configured for the air-superiority role, this F-15C-25-MC (79-0047) from the 36th TFW flys formation with a KC-135. Position of air intake is noteworthy.

tractor (Cat I) aircraft and its absence would have less of an impact on the test program (in fact, it was an un-needed attrition aircraft); and since F17 was just rolling down the production line fewer things would have to be ''undone''. The aircraft was modified by McAir between April 27 and June 11, 1974 for the tests by deleting all non-mission critical systems including: the flap and speed brake actuators; internal armament; the radar and fire-control system; non-critical cockpit displays and radios; one of the generators; the utility hydraulic system; and, of course, the 50 lbs. of paint (hence its name). Additions included: a revised oxygen system; support equipment for the full pressure suit worn by the pilots; extra batteries; a long pitot boom with alpha and beta vanes; an over-the-shoulder video camera; a battery powered radio; sensitive g meters; a standby attitude gyro; a large VHF antenna under the canopy behind the pilot; and a special ''hold-down'' device in place of the tail hook. The final result was an aircraft that weighed 1,800 lbs. less than the other block-6 aircraft. When weighed in preparation for a 30,000 meter run (on test flight #37), 72-119 weighed 36,799 lbs. Simulations, primarily of the high altitude profiles, were run between May 3 - September 30 and the application to the Federation Aeronautique Internationale (FAI) was made on September 15, 1974. The flight profile for the 30,000 meter (98,425 ft.) record was as follows:

- Release from the hold-down cable at full afterburner with 7,000 lbs. of fuel
- Gear up and rotate at 70 knots (3 seconds after release!)
- At 420 knots, rotate vertically into an Immelmann and hold 2.65 g
- Expect to arrive level, upside down, at 32,000 ft. and 1.1 Mach
- Rotate to right side up, accelerate to 600 knots while climbing to 36,000 ft.
- Accelerate to 2.25 Mach and pull 4.0 g to a 60° climb angle
- Hold 60° climb
- Shut down the afterburners when they quit
- Shut down the engines whey they flame-out
- Ride ballistically over the top at 55 knots and 103,000 ft.
- Descend at a 55° dive angle
- When below 55,000 ft., try to start the engines
- Go Home.

The record runs were accomplished at Grand Forks AFB, North Dakota, where the cold atmospheric conditions were ideal. Six different record flights were flown (there were several unsuccessful ones in between), and margins of between 15% and 33% were achieved over the previous records. For the record attempts the aircraft was physically held-down to the runway while full power was applied. The actual records set by *Streak Eagle* were:

Altitude (meters)	Date	Pilot	Old Record (secs.)	Goal (secs.)	Actual (secs.)
3,000	1/16/75	Smith	34.50	27.00	27.57
6,000	1/16/75	Macfarlane	48.80	38.60	39.33
9,000	1/16/75	Macfarlane	61.70	47.90	48.86
12,000	1/16/75	Macfarlane	77.10	58.00	59.38
15,000	1/16/75	Peterson	114.50	73.70	77.02
20,000	1/19/75	Smith	169.80	126.10	122.94
25,000	1/26/75	Peterson	192.60	163.70	161.02
30,000	2/1/75	Smith	243.90	206.90	207.80

A highly modified MiG-25 (E-266) since has retaken several of the higher altitude records, and also set one to 35,000 meters, although it is still a matter of some controversy over whether it was rocket assisted. There was consideration given to further modifying *Streak Eagle*, including using more powerful production engines, and making another attempt, but this never materialized. Like the other Category II test aircraft, 72-119 was to have been brought up to production standards and sent to an operational squadron, however the sale of four of the eight aircraft to Israel, and the amount of work needed on F17, made this impractical, and the plan was abandoned. *Streak Eagle* since has been turned over to the Air Force Museum where, to protect it from corrosion, it has been painted in a *Compass Ghost* scheme utilizing two tones of blue instead of the normal gray.

CONSTRUCTION AND SYSTEMS:

COCKPIT

Crew of one (A and C) or two in tandem (B, D, and E), on McDonnell Douglas IC-7 (through block-17 and all

Israeli) or ACES-II (block-18 and subsequent, except Israeli) ejection seats. The ACES-II ejection seat automatically selects one of three ejection modes: mode 1 is a low speed mode during which the parachute is deployed almost immediately after the seat departs the aircraft; mode 2 is a high speed mode during which a drogue chute is first deployed to slow the seat, followed by the deployment of the main parachute; mode 3 is a high altitude mode in which the sequence of events is the same as mode 2 except that man-seat separation is delayed until a safe altitude is reached. There are two ejection control handles, one mounted on each forward upper side of the seat. The controls are interconnected so that actuation of either control initiates ejection. A ten minute supply of emergency oxygen is furnished by a storage bottle on the left rear of the ejection seat, and is activated automatically upon ejection. Later aircraft have a system called SEAWARS installed that automatically releases the parachute risers from the pilot upon immersion in sea water.

The single piece wrap-around windscreen provides 10% more viewing area and a 32% weight reduction compared to a three-piece design. The windscreen is made of fusion bonded cast acrylic outer layers and a polycarbonate center layer. The bubble type canopy is made of 0.29 in. thick polycarbonate with an abrasion resistant coating. This material is 29% lighter than laminated Plexiglas, and 56% lighter than laminated tempered safety glass. The canopy is made of two pieces, with a small frame separating the two pieces just aft of the pilot's head, since there is not a production capability to form such a large object from one piece. The two-seater's canopy has different contours to provide additional headroom for the second crew member. Retractable boarding steps are provided on the left side of the aircraft, although they are seldom used.

McDonnell Douglas Electronics Company builds the HUD, which projects all essential flight information in the form of symbols onto a combining glass positioned above the instrument panel at the pilot's eye level. The HUD's field of vision is approximately 20° by 20°. The display presents the information needed to conduct flight operations and to intercept and engage targets without the need to look inside the cockpit. The HUD continuously

*A fully configured air-superiority **F-15** displays a centerline 610 gal. fuel tank, four AIM-7 "Sparrow III" and four AIM-9 "Sidewinder" air-to-air missiles. The natural metal finish around the engine compartment and the absence of "turkey feathers" on the engine exhausts are noteworthy. Snag tooth horizontal stabilizers and raked wingtips are evident.*

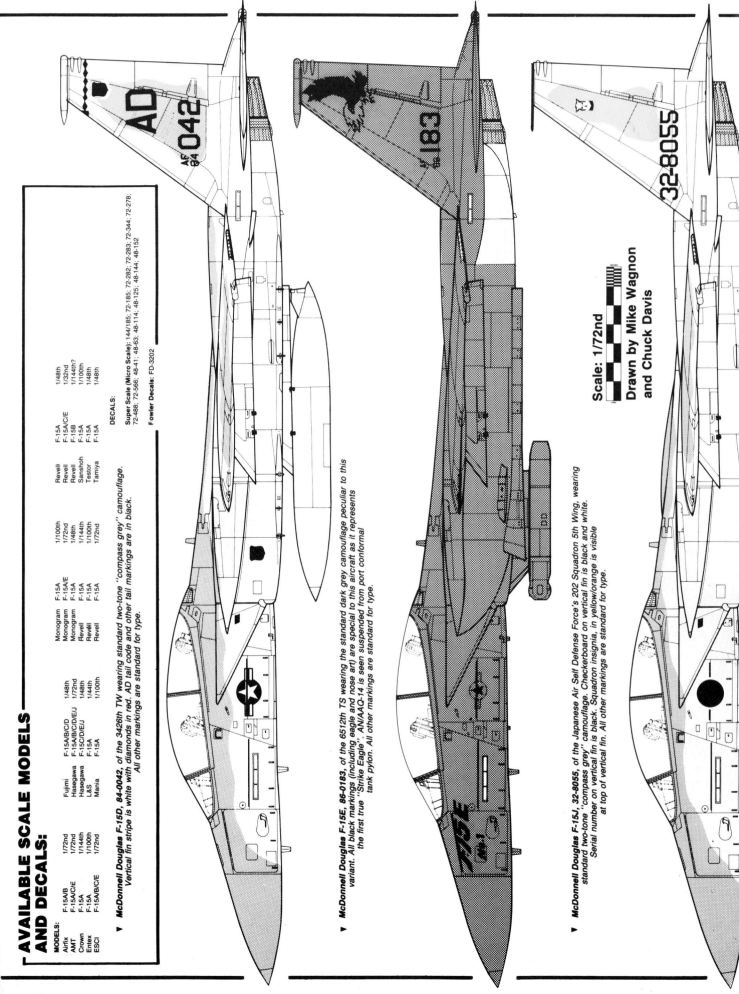

AVAILABLE SCALE MODELS AND DECALS:

MODELS:

Airfix	F-15A/B	1/72nd	Fujimi	F-15A/B/C/D	1/48th	Monogram	F-15A/B/C/D	1/100th
AMT	F-15A/C/E	1/72nd	Hasegawa	F-15A/B/C/D/E/J	1/72nd
Crown	F-15A	1/144th	Hasegawa	F-15C/D/E/J	1/48th
Entex	F-15A	1/100th	L&S	F-15A	1/44th
ESCI	F-15A/B/C/E		Mania	F-15A	1/100th

Monogram	F-15A	1/100th	Revell	F-15A	1/48th
Monogram	F-15A/E	1/72nd	Revell	F-15A/C/E	1/32nd
Monogram	F-15A	1/48th	Revell	F-15B	1/144th?
Revell	F-15A	1/144th	Sanshoh	F-15A	1/100th
Revell	F-15A	1/100th	Testor	F-15A	1/48th
Revell	F-15A	1/72nd	Tamiya	F-15A	1/48th

DECALS:

Super Scale (Micro Scale): 144/185; 72-185; 72-282; 72-283; 72-344; 72-278; 72-488; 72-566; 48-41; 48-63; 48-114; 48-125; 48-144; 48-152

Fowler Decals: FD-3202

▼ **McDonnell Douglas F-15D, 84-0042,** of the 3426th TW wearing standard two-tone "compass grey" camouflage. Vertical fin stripe is white with diamonds in red. AD tail code and other tail markings are in black. All other markings are standard for type.

▼ **McDonnell Douglas F-15E, 86-0183,** of the 6512th TS wearing the standard dark grey camouflage peculiar to this variant. All black markings (including eagle and nose art) are special to this aircraft as it represents the first true "Strike Eagle". AN/AAQ-14 is seen suspended from port conformal tank pylon. All other markings are standard for type.

▼ **McDonnell Douglas F-15J, 32-8055,** of the Japanese Air Self Defense Force's 202 Squadron 5th Wing, wearing standard two-tone "compass grey" camouflage. Checkerboard on vertical fin is black and white. Squadron insignia, in yellow/orange is visible at top of vertical fin. Serial number on vertical fin is black. All other markings are standard for type.

Scale: 1/72nd

Drawn by Mike Wagnon and Chuck Davis

SELECT MARKINGS

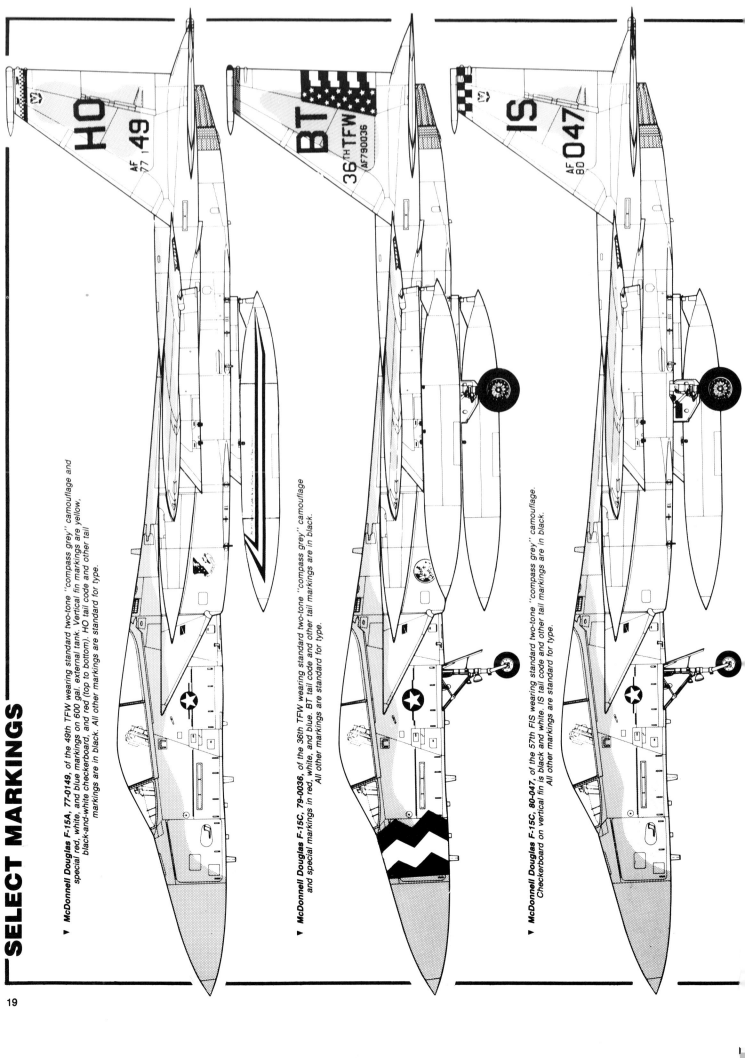

▶ *McDonnell Douglas F-15A, 77-0149, of the 49th TFW wearing standard two-tone "compass grey" camouflage and special red, white, and blue markings on 600 gal. external tank. Vertical fin markings are yellow, black-and-white checkerboard, and red (top to bottom). HO tail code and other tail markings are in black. All other markings are standard for type.*

▶ *McDonnell Douglas F-15C, 79-0036, of the 36th TFW wearing standard two-tone "compass grey" camouflage and special markings in red, white, and blue. BT tail code and other tail markings are in black. All other markings are standard for type.*

▶ *McDonnell Douglas F-15C, 80-047, of the 57th FIS wearing standard two-tone "compass grey" camouflage. Checkerboard on vertical fin is black and white. IS tail code and other tail markings are in black. All other markings are standard for type.*

The second **TF-15A (later F-15B) 71-291** during an early development flight with FAST Packs. Note the glossy underside finish (reflection of AIM-7 on lower wing). The upper fuselage and wings were painted flat air-superiority blue. Many prototypes had the da-glo orange applied since the air-superiority blue blended into Edwards' sky.

The 350th **F-15C (85-0125)** on the McAir assembly line. The different colors of the various alloys used in making the skin panels are noteworthy. At this stage the wings are being attached to the center fuselage which in turn is attached to the forward and aft fuselage sections. The horizontal stabilators are attached at the next assembly line station.

An **F-15A-15-MC (76-0008)** assigned to the 318th FIS at McChord AFB, Washington. The Air Defense TAC (ADTAC) squadrons had the most colorful markings of any F-15 units, with the 318th being the most faithful to their traditional design. Most ADTAC squadrons have since deleted all color from their markings and adopted gray-on-gray schemes.

18

*This 32nd TFS **F-15A-18-MC (77-0082)** is fully armed for an intercept mission, with a 610 gal. fuel tank, four AIM-7s and four AIM-9s. Note the small ECM antennas under the forward fuselage and on top of the left vertical stabilizer. Also note early-style national insignia. The 32nd TFS now operates late model F-15C/Ds equipped with CFTs.*

*Two **F-15Cs** from the 18th TFW at Kadena AB, Okinawa. Color of aerial refueling slipway door in left wing root is noteworthy. The air intakes are shown in a partially down position, exposing a small amount of unpainted surface along their back edge where they pivot. Each aircraft carries a training AIM-9 "Sidewinder" on the wing pylon.*

*An **F-15C-29-MC (80-0040)** assigned to the 57th FIS at Keflavik, Iceland intercepts a Tu-95 "Bear". This squadron operates F-15Cs equipped with Conformal Fuel Tanks to extend their interception range. Note the live AIM-7 "Sparrow III" on the forward left CFT station. The 57th does not wrap the checkerboard stripe to the inside of the vertical stabilizer.*

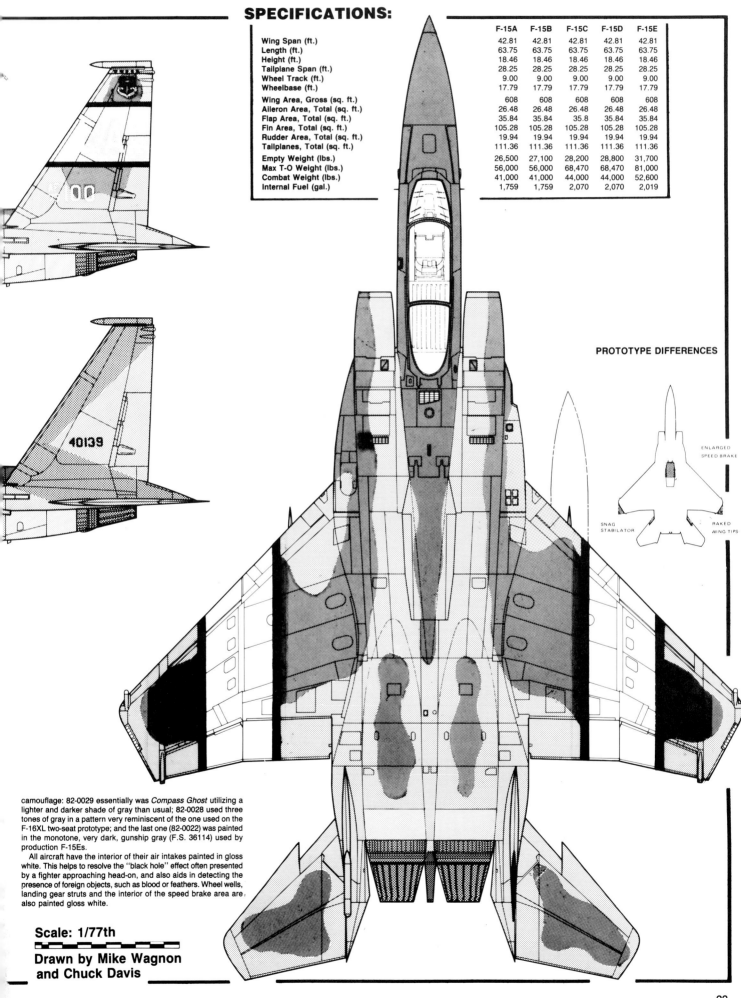

SPECIFICATIONS:

	F-15A	F-15B	F-15C	F-15D	F-15E
Wing Span (ft.)	42.81	42.81	42.81	42.81	42.81
Length (ft.)	63.75	63.75	63.75	63.75	63.75
Height (ft.)	18.46	18.46	18.46	18.46	18.46
Tailplane Span (ft.)	28.25	28.25	28.25	28.25	28.25
Wheel Track (ft.)	9.00	9.00	9.00	9.00	9.00
Wheelbase (ft.)	17.79	17.79	17.79	17.79	17.79
Wing Area, Gross (sq. ft.)	608	608	608	608	608
Aileron Area, Total (sq. ft.)	26.48	26.48	26.48	26.48	26.48
Flap Area, Total (sq. ft.)	35.84	35.84	35.8	35.84	35.84
Fin Area, Total (sq. ft.)	105.28	105.28	105.28	105.28	105.28
Rudder Area, Total (sq. ft.)	19.94	19.94	19.94	19.94	19.94
Tailplanes, Total (sq. ft.)	111.36	111.36	111.36	111.36	111.36
Empty Weight (lbs.)	26,500	27,100	28,200	28,800	31,700
Max T-O Weight (lbs.)	56,000	56,000	68,470	68,470	81,000
Combat Weight (lbs.)	41,000	41,000	44,000	44,000	52,600
Internal Fuel (gal.)	1,759	1,759	2,070	2,070	2,019

PROTOTYPE DIFFERENCES

ENLARGED SPEED BRAKE

SNAG STABILATOR

RAKED WING TIPS

camouflage: 82-0029 essentially was *Compass Ghost* utilizing a lighter and darker shade of gray than usual; 82-0028 used three tones of gray in a pattern very reminiscent of the one used on the F-16XL two-seat prototype; and the last one (82-0022) was painted in the monotone, very dark, gunship gray (F.S. 36114) used by production F-15Es.

All aircraft have the interior of their air intakes painted in gloss white. This helps to resolve the ''black hole'' effect often presented by a fighter approaching head-on, and also aids in detecting the presence of foreign objects, such as blood or feathers. Wheel wells, landing gear struts and the interior of the speed brake area are also painted gloss white.

Scale: 1/77th

Drawn by Mike Wagnon and Chuck Davis

MCDONNELL DOUGLAS F-15A, 73-0100

▼ *McDonnell Douglas F-15A, 73-0100, of the 55th TFS, 58th TFW, wearing standard two-tone "compass grey" camouflage. The vertical fin and wing stripes are in yellow with black borders. The vertical fin tip stripe is green with five white stars. Vertical fin badge is standard Tactical Air Command, and the unit badge is visible on the intake cheek. LA tail code and serial numbers are in white.*

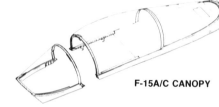

F-15A/C CANOPY

T AND MARKINGS

first 42 F-15s (71-280/291, 72-113/120, 73-085/099, /114) were painted in "air-superiority" blue, with the excep-71-287 which was finished in gloss white for its role as the st aircraft, and 72-119 (*Streak Eagle*) which was not painted. periority Blue (officially simply "Superiority Blue") consisted upper surfaces being painted in a gloss AS Blue (F.S. 35450) e lower surfaces getting flat AS Blue (F.S. 15450). This paint e was considered effective in the clear blue skies over ds and Luke, but it was not so effective in cloudy skies, such e expected to be encountered over Europe most of the year.

▼ *McDonnell Douglas F-15B, 74-0139, of the 58th TFW, in unusual, short-lived Keith Ferris-developed camouflage pattern of light grey (F.S. 36440), medium grey (F.S. 36231), and dark grey (F.S. 36118). Noteworthy are missing national insigne, "false canopy", and small serial number presented as "40089".*

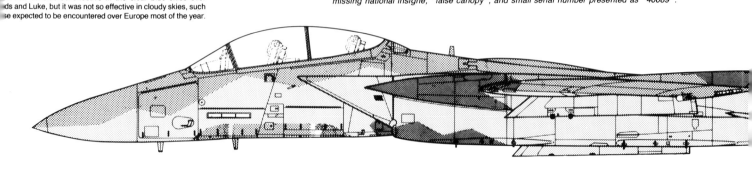

majority of the test aircraft received dayglo orange mark-their wingtips, vertical and horizontal stabilizers and engine to make them more visible during test flights. Several Cat aft have been repainted into a gloss white with contrasting blue or bright red) trim during their later use as McAir test t. The first F-15B (71-290) later received a colorful red, white, ue paint scheme for its role as the F-15S/MTD. The second (71-291) also received a red, white, and blue scheme, this duplicate of one developed for (but never used by) the erbirds air demonstration squadron. The aircraft was painted late 1975 to celebrate the U.S. Bicentennial and later went world-tour in a slightly modified version of the scheme. raft up to and including 72-113 had a black tip on the radome Aircraft beginning with 72-114 used blue trips that more y resembled the rest of the paint scheme. Early *Compass* aircraft still had light blue tips before gray tips reached the ction line. Some test aircraft sported long test instrumenta-ooms from the front of all-metal noses at various times in careers.

the Air Superiority Blue operational aircraft were repainted *Compass Ghost* during their first depot level maintenance . It should also be noted that the tail codes initially used at were painted in white, instead of the more normal black. The tion to this was 73-109, the second aircraft to arrive, which lack tail codes for several months before having them re-d in white. Operational squadrons use black tail codes, (also dopted by Luke), although some Nellis aircraft are periodical-n with white tail codes.
production aircraft after 73-100 (74-0137 for two-seaters), in-g foreign deliveries, have been painted in "*Compass Ghost*". t *Compass Ghost* has been a continuing effort by the military the most effective camouflage scheme possible. The cur--15 scheme consists of two shades of gray, called Light Ghost

Gray (F.S. 36320) and Dark Ghost Gray (F.S. 36375), applied in a pattern designed to minimize the visual reflectance of various contours of the aircraft. Three different operational aircraft at Luke also received high-visibility markings for a short time during 1976: 73-100 sported wide yellow bands around the wings and tails; 73-103 got alternating white and red "invasion stripes" around the forward fuselage and wings; while 73-112 received similar (but not identical) stripes in black. Additionally, 74-113 was painted in standard *Compass Ghost* with a F.S. 36118 false-canopy on the bottom of the fuselage.

Four aircraft were painted in the "Ferris Attitude Deceptive" scheme dreamed up by aviation artist Keith Ferris. This scheme reintroduced the concept of painting an aircraft to make it difficult to determine its direction of movement during close-in aerial combat. The scheme also was applied to several F-14s, as well as both AF and Navy F-4s and aggressor aircraft. An additional feature of the concept was a "false-canopy" painted on the aircraft bottom. There were several legal concerns over the continued use of the paint scheme by the military, and the aircraft were repainted into *Compass Ghost* during late-1976. The following Federal Standard (F.S.) colors were used by the Ferris aircraft:

s/n	Light	Medium	Dark	Canopy
73-111	36440	36231	36118	36118
74-0089	36440	36231	36320	36118
74-0110	36622	36440	36231	36231
74-0139	36440	36231	36118	36118

The *Strike Eagle* prototype (71-291) originally was painted in *Compass Ghost*, then was repainted in the standard "*European One*" scheme of dark gray (F.S. 36081) and two dark greens (F.S. 34092 and F.S. 34102). Three F-15Cs assigned to the 57th FWW at Nellis were painted in different schemes to find the final F-15E

*The first **F-15E (86-0183)** on a test flight. The AN/ALQ-135B antenna on the right rear fuselage extension near the trailing edge of the horizontal stabilizer and the FLIR/LANTIRN pod under the air intake are noteworthy. Later production F-15Es have an antenna on both rear fuselage extensions. Aft formation light strip on F-15Es differ from early F-15s.*

*Painted up in the "World Tour" scheme, the second **F-15B (71-291)** is rigged for air-to-ground delivery tests. Cameras attached to the outer wing panels and under the rear fuselage to record weapon separation are noteworthy. CFTs are of the early type-1 configuration. This paint scheme was developed for but never used by the "Thunderbirds".*

*The first **F-15B (71-290)** is rolled out as the STOL/Maneuver Technology Demonstrator (STOL/MTD). Two-dimensional exhaust nozzles and forward canards are noteworthy. STOL Demo should show significant performance improvements, especially during take-off and landings. This aircraft is scheduled to conduct reverse-thrust tests during November 1989.*

displays the following information: magnetic heading, indicated airspeed, barometric altitude, velocity vector, aircraft load factor (g), and indicated Mach number. Additional information is presented depending upon the mode (air-to-air, air-to-ground, landing, etc.) selected. The HUD in the F-15E is of an improved, wide field of vision (25° by 40°) design, though it displays essentially the same information as the earlier units.

The front cockpit of the two-seat models is identical to the cockpit on the single-seater with the addition of an intercom control panel. The F-15A/B and early F-15C/Ds contain conventional flight and weapons instrumentation. The MSIP-II program added a Sperry multi-purpose color display (MPCD) and programmable armament control set (PACS) to the cockpit of the F-15C/D to replace the original armament control panel. This screen also is capable of displaying video images from a long-range optics system (yet to be installed in any F-15s), or video presentations from some weapons. The rear cockpit of the F-15B/D/E contains flight controls and reduced (essential) flight instrumentation. Both cockpits are illuminated with blue filtered white lighting which is preferred over red lighting because white maintains high legibility to lower light levels and also allows color coding of displays. Light intensity can be adjusted for each display.

The F-15E contains four multi-purpose displays (MPD) and three multi-purpose color displays (MPCD). There are two MPDs in each cockpit, one MPCD in the front cockpit and two MPCDs in the rear cockpit. The MPDs display system data, sensor video and weapon information in a monochromatic format. The MPDs have 20 peripheral pushbuttons by which the crew can control weapons systems, sensors and data to be displayed. Legends are positioned adjacent to each pushbutton to advise the crew of the modes and options selectable for operation of the onboard radar, FLIR, navigation, and weapons systems. The exact content of the data in the display formats is software programmable. The MPCDs display monochromatic or multicolor presentation of sensor and weapon video overlaid with symbology, advisory readouts, and navigation data. Color coding of display data aids in quick interpretation of complex formats. Color presentation of navigational maps also contributes to easy and accurate assessment of the tactical situation. The MPCDs also have 20 peripheral pushbuttons which provide control in the same manner as the MPD. Each MPD/MPCD has a power switch, a brightness control, and a built-in test indicator. The contents and organization of the various displays can be controlled by the multi-purpose switch on the forward control stick, or the rear right hand controller.

The front cockpit control stick consists of a stick grip and force transducer, and contains six (seven in the F-15E) controls: an autopilot/nose gear steering disengage switch (paddle switch); nose gear steering/weapons button; a trigger; a weapon release button; a trim switch; an auto acquisition button; and a castle switch to control the FLIR (F-15E only). The rear cockpit stick has only four controls: an autopilot/nose gear steering disengage switch (paddle switch); a weapons release button; a trim switch and a refueling release button. The rear cockpit trigger, although present, is non-functional. The front throttles contain switches for: rudder trim; flap actuation; microphone; speed brake actuation; undesignate/missile rejection; weapon/mode; target designation and antenna elevation. The F-15C and F-15E added a switch to control the chaff/flare dispenser. The F-15E also added switches for laser designator control, and a multi-purpose switch. The rear throttles provide controls for rudder trim, speed brake actuation and the microphone. The rear cockpit of the F-15E also contains a hand controller on the forward inboard section of the left and right consoles. These controllers are used to provide sensor/display control. Both controllers contain a trigger switch, a laser designator switch, a target designate switch and a "coolie" switch. The left controller also contains a castle switch to control the FLIR, a chaff/flare dispenser set control switch and a mode reject switch. The right controller also contains an interrogate switch, a multi-purpose switch and an auto-acquisition switch.

In addition to the normal caution and warning lights contained on the instrument panel and HUD, the F-15 is equipped with a voice warning system that can announce some emergencies (fire, low fuel, etc.) to the pilot over the intercom system. On block-24 (79-0004) and subsequent aircraft, a video tape recording system is installed with the capability of recording the display on either the HUD or the vertical situation display. Maximum recording time is 30 minutes. This system replaced the

This 32nd TFS F-15D-24-MC (79-0004) from Soesterberg AB in the Netherlands is liberally adorned with nose art. Tail stripe is orange with black borders and is positioned somewhat lower than stateside units.

This F-15C-28-MC (80-0027) is used by the Commander of the 94th TFS as evidenced by the non-standard tail markings. This aircraft is fitted with all known ECM antennas under nose and on top of the left vertical stabilizer.

F-15Cs assigned to the 57th FIS at Keflavik, Iceland regularly fly with type-1 CFTs to increase their intercept radius. Intercepts are normally flown with two AIM-9 missiles. Size of the checkerboard stripe on tail is noteworthy.

The CO of the 1st TFW uses this F-15C-29-MC (80-0051) with unusual tail markings. The chevrons on the top of the fin are the colors (yellow, red, and blue) of the three squadrons assigned to the 1st TFW.

*The second prototype **F-15A (71-281)** was turned over to the NASA Dryden Flight Research Center on January 5, 1981, looking decidedly worse for wear. Note the reference marks on the forward fuselage to determine the angle of the air intakes. The aircraft briefly participated in several NASA test programs before being retired during 1983.*

*The third prototype **(71-282)** being processed into MASDC at Davis-Monthan AFB during April 1978. Note the unconventional location of formation lights on the vertical stabilizers. There was not a set on the other side, but two were located on top of the fuselage near the speed brake. Personnel assigned to the AECS program signed above the pitot tube.*

*The sixth prototype **(71-285)** has been repainted (along with several others) into this flashy white and blue scheme. The matching fuel tank is noteworthy. The aircraft is used for continuing flight test work and public relations appearances at airshows. This aircraft was used for weapons systems trials and was nicknamed "Killer" during Category I testing.*

The spin test prototype *(71-287)* before being bailed to NASA. This was the only prototype originally painted white, which was done to aid in photography during spin recovery testing. A spin-recovery parachute container was mounted on top of the fuselage between the vertical stabilizers. Testing was accomplished with a variety of pylon configurations.

During the latter part of April 1976 the second *TF-15A (71-291)* was painted in Armée de l'Air markings during demonstrations to French pilots. Flags of the various other countries to receive F-15 demonstrations were painted on the forward fuselage under the cockpit. The aircraft remained in these markings for approximately ten days.

The *F-15A-6-MC (72-119)* assigned to project "Streak Eagle" stopped at Buckley ANGB during December 1974 prior to the time-to-climb altitude attempts. During February 1975 this aircraft would climb to 30,000 meters (roughly 100,000 ft.) in 207 sec. from brake release. The small balancers on top of the vertical stabilizers are noteworthy.

Brian Rogers

This F-15C-34-MC (82-0031) is used by the 57th FWW CO. The tailcode is highlighted with white, as is the wing number. Early Nellis aircraft used white tailcodes instead of the current black markings.

16mm film-based KB-27B HUD camera system installed on aircraft prior to block-24. The KB-27B system was installed forward and to the right of the HUD and recorded the combined HUD symbology and forward field of vision. A 100 ft. film capacity magazine was provided. The oxygen system includes a 10 liter liquid oxygen supply with a normal system operating pressure of 70 psi.

FUSELAGE

The F-15's fuselage is built in three sections, primarily for ease of manufacturing. All three sections are all-metal, semi-monocoque structures, constructed primarily of aluminum with some titanium in high-stress areas. The forward fuselage is built to enhance accessibility to the avionics, and contains 90% of the black boxes and 85% of the wiring. Six non-structural doors are provided to access the avionics. The center fuselage contains the mechanical parts of the M61 cannon, the 20mm ammunition drum, and fuel cells. A truss structure allows the wing load to be carried around the engine air ducts, permitting a lower weight, smaller cross-section configuration. The wing torque box is a multi-cell, three-spar, structure utilizing multi-stiffened skins to carry the bending loads into the fuselage through three pairs of pinned lugs. To increase aft fuselage structural efficiency, engine removal/installation is made from the rear of the aircraft, with the engines sliding on rails contained on each side of each engine bay. The engines are separated by a keeled titanium web which supports the arresting hook. The keel also protects the second engine from damage caused by a catastrophic failure of the first, enhancing survivability. A fire extinguishing system is fitted in both engine bays, a first for an American fighter.

The special nose radome was developed by Brunswick Corporation, Technical Products Division. It is constructed from a synthetic foam material sandwiched between outer skins and features a weight savings of 35% in comparison with earlier radome structures. It also provides heat resistance up to 500° F., and an undistorted passage for radar signals. A small AN/ALQ-135B antenna radome is mounted on the right fuselage extension just aft of the base of the right rudder on F-15C/D aircraft and F-15Es carry a similar radome on both sides. Six small antennas are carried on the underside of the nose, from front to rear: TACAN/UHF blade antenna; two AN/ALQ-135 band-2 antennas; UHF blade antenna; AN/ALR-56 low-band antenna on the front nose gear door; and an AN/ALQ-135 band-1 antenna just aft of the nose landing gear. A UHF/VHF communications antenna is located on the upper fuselage, just behind the cockpit. To simplify maintenance access, the F-15 has 185 access doors and panels covering a total of 570 sq. ft. on its wings and fuselage, 85% of which can be reached without work stands.

A speed brake on the upper center-fuselage is constructed of graphite-epoxy, aluminum honeycomb and titanium. It is electrically controlled and hydraulically operated. The speed brake can be positioned to any intermediate position between fully retracted and fully extended if the angle of attack is below 25 units. If the AOA is above 25 units, the speed brake will not extend if selected. Three different styles of speed brakes have been used: the first twenty aircraft (71-280/291, 72-113/120) used a 20 sq. ft. rectangular speed brake that was found to cause a mild buffeting at some airspeeds; the first 30 production aircraft (73-085/114) used a 31.5 sq. ft. speed brake with an external stiffener; while aircraft beginning with block-10 (74-081) use an identical speed brake without the external stiffener. The newer speed brake extension angle was limited to 25° on aircraft prior to block-13, but was increased to 45° by TCTO 1F-15A-734 and on block-13 (75-0018) and later aircraft. Some block-7 through block-9 aircraft have been retrofitted with the later speed brake without the external stiffener during depot level maintenance. The last block of F-15As and all F-15C/D/Es had a slight change in contours to the area immediately behind the speed brake to simplify production. Apparently no F-15Bs were built to the newer design.

Integrally machined aluminum and titanium are used throughout the F-15 to reduce weight and cost. This construction technique eliminates many of the joints common to the build-up construction of earlier types. The F-15E's upper rear fuselage, rear fuselage keel, main landing gear doors, and some rear fuselage fairings incorporate superplastic formed/diffusion bonded (SPF/DB) titanium structure. The fairing extending between the engine nozzles was deleted from the F-15E during the redesign of the aft fuselage.

WINGS

One of the major factors involved in allowing one aircraft to develop more lift in a turn than another is the wing loading. The other major factor is having enough thrust to overcome the additional drag generated during maneuvering. The air that spills from under the wing to the lower pressure on top of the wing disrupts the airflow and increasingly degrades the lifting capability as the angle of attack increases. This degradation is known as induced drag because it is induced by lift itself. In the years that had followed the development of the F-86, designers had purposely reduced the wing area to lower drag and enable higher top speeds. While this looked good on paper, experience had shown that few, if any, dogfights took place above 1.2 Mach, and none had ever occurred at 2.0 Mach. The trade-off studies on the F-15 wing were designed around a lift-to-drag (L/D) ratio optimized for dogfighting in transonic and high subsonic speeds. Unfortunately, there was very little data available in this area since the last time any research had been done in support of the F-86 project. McAir ended by keeping three wind tunnels busy for the better part of a year, and the ultimate wing was selected from some 800 analyzed configurations, with 107 of these tested in the wind tunnels. This wing was the antithesis of what the F-4 wing had been, containing no high-lift devices (slats, etc.), and control surfaces consisting of only simple ailerons and two-position flaps. The F-15 would spend 10,150 hours in the wind tunnel during its early development, in contrast to the F-4, which had spent just under 4,000.

The wings are shoulder mounted with a NACA-64A airfoil section of varying thickness-to-chord ratios, ranging from 6.6% at the root, to 3.0% at the tip. A total of 608 sq. ft. of wing area is provided (six less than the original wingtip design). The leading edges have a conical camber, and there are no leading edge lift devices. The wing has 1° of anhedral, and 0° of incidence. Sweepback is 45° at the leading edge, and 38°42' at quarter-chord. The wing is a fail-safe structure comprised of a torque-box with integrally stiffened machined skins and conventionally machined ribs, both of light alloy and titanium. Three titanium main spars are provided, and the aircraft can continue flying (but not maneuvering) with any one of these severed. Leading and trailing edges are of conventional light alloy rib and skin construction. The wingtips are of aluminum honeycomb construction. No spoilers, trim tabs, or anti-ice system are fitted.

A single aileron outboard and flap section inboard are hydraulically operated by National Water Lift actuators. Each wing has a two-position flap with 35.84 sq. ft. of area and a straight trailing edge. The flaps are electrically controlled and hydraulically operated. When the flaps are down, they are protected from structural damage by a blow-up airspeed switch which is set to automatically retract the flaps at approximately 250 KIAS. The ailerons each have an area of 26.48 sq. ft., and have a swept back trailing edge. Wing loading at combat weight is extremely low for a modern fighter, at approximately 56 lbs. per sq. ft. of effective lifting surface (not necessarily just the wing). Antennas for the AN/ALR-56 radar warning receiver are located on the leading edge of each wingtip, just inboard of the position lights. Low voltage electro-luminescent formation lights are located on the tapered portion of the wingtip.

TAIL SURFACES

Twin vertical stabilizers are of cantilever construction making extensive use of boron-epoxy and honeycomb composite materials. The fins have 36°34' of sweep on their leading edge, and provide 125.22 sq. ft. of area, including rudders. The vertical tails are identical and are interchangeable, as are the horizontal stabilizers. The mechanical aileron-rudder interconnect (ARI) adjusts the control system such that lateral stick motion results in varying rudder deflection dependent on longitudinal stick position. With the stick aft of neutral, lateral motion causes rudder deflection in the same direction as stick motion. With the stick forward of neutral, later stick motion causes rudder deflection in the opposite direction. In addition, if flaps are down, the amount of rudder deflection for a given lateral input is increased. Rudder servo actuators are manufactured by Ronson Hydraulic Units Corporation.

The vertical fins have been capped with pods of differing configurations. The twenty test and some early production aircraft had dummy pods on both tails, with the left pod having an angled aft section, and the right's terminating abruptly, although these got mixed and matched periodically. Later production aircraft have a larger pod on the left that contains antennas for the AN/ALQ-128 ECM system, and the right fin is capped with a harmonic mass balancer only. Some early aircraft have been retrofitted with an ECM-style pod on the left fin, but still retain the dummy pod on the right. A few aircraft have been seen with later style ECM-style pods on both fins. The production F-15s acquired by Israel and Japan have mass balancers on top of both fins, although some Japanese aircraft have been seen with a modified ECM-style pod on top of the left fin, presumably containing components of the J/ALQ-8 ECM system. Some aircraft procured by Saudi Arabia carry an ECM-style pod on the left fin, but it is unclear what system is installed since the AN/ALQ-128 has not been released to any foreign users.

There are two small fairings on the trailing edge near the top of each vertical tail. The upper fairing contains a receiving antenna for the AN/ALR-56 radar warning system, while the lower fairing houses position lights. During late 1987, a corrosion problem around the attach point for the vertical stabilizer was discovered on older F-15s, and McAir and the AF currently are investigating to determine how widespread the damage is, and what can be done to correct the problem.

The all-flying horizontal stabilators have a dog-tooth leading edge, with extended chord outboard. The leading edge sweepback is 50° and a total of 111.36 sq. ft. of area is provided. The stabilators are capable of symmetrical or differential movement, with the leading edge capable of ±20° of deflection. Longitudinal control stick motion positions the stabilators symmetrically to provide pitch control. The pitch ratio is automatically adjusted for altitude and speed. The ratio is high at low speeds, and low at high speeds or low altitude. If hydraulic pressure is lost, the pitch ratio will drive to an intermediate position and lock. If the mechanical linkage becomes jammed, mechanical longitudinal control is lost; however, the control augmentation system can provide enough stabilator control for moderate flight maneuvers and landing. Actuators for the stabilators are made by National Water Lift Company. Boost and pitch compensators for the control stick are furnished by Moog, Inc.

LANDING GEAR

All F-15s use an electrically controlled, hydraulically operated, tricycle type landing gear with a single wheel on each unit. All units retract forward, and incorporate oleo-pneumatic shock absorbers made by Cleveland Pneumatic Tool Company. The nosewheel and 22 x

6.6-10 tire are made by Goodyear. The tire is inflated to 260 psi. The main wheels are by Bendix, with 34.5 x 9.75-18 tires supplied by Goodyear and inflated to 340 psi. Bendix carbon heat-sink brakes with a Hydro-Aire anti-skid system are fitted to the main gear. The anti-skid system is not considered effective below 30 knots, and heavy braking is not recommended below that speed. After the main and nose gear are extended, the forward doors are closed (it was common to see the main gear doors open on the initial development aircraft). A nosewheel steering system is provided, and is automatically engaged when weight is on the nosewheel. Normal steering authority is ±15°, with a maneuvering mode allowing ±45°. An emergency system provides hydraulic accumulator pressure to power the brakes in the event the normal hydraulic system is lost. Anti-skid is not available with the emergency system.

Due to its significantly higher gross weight, the F-15E uses Bendix wheels and Michelin AIR-X radial tires on all three units. Nosewheel tire size is 22 x 7.75-9 and the main units use a 36 x 11-18 tire. All are inflated to 305 psi. The main landing gear doors of the F-15E have a noticeable bulge in order to accommodate the larger wheel/tire assemblies.

A retractable arresting hook is enclosed in the underside of the aft fuselage. It is electrically controlled, extended by gravity and a hydraulic dashpot, and retracted by utility hydraulic pressure. F-15A/B aircraft prior to block-15 had doors to cover the arresting hook in its retracted position, but these were removed, along with their associated mechanisms, by TCTO 1F-15A-764 dated May 13, 1977. Block-15 and later aircraft never had the doors installed. Removal of the doors was undertaken primarily because it was deemed that the small increase in drag was more than offset by simplified maintenance. The tail hook on the F-15E is of a new design to handle the significant increase in gross weight of that variant.

AMAD/JFS

The F-15's generators and hydraulic pumps are attached to an airframe mounted accessory drive (AMAD) unit. This unit receives power from the engines via two drive shafts, and contains four hydraulic pumps and two integrated drive generators (IDG). The IDGs provide ac power and are rated at 40/50 Kva each. The jet fuel starter (JFS), a self contained auxiliary power unit, is mounted between the engines and is connected to the AMAD for ground power. The JFS gives the F-15 a self-starting capability, and can start either engine, but not both simultaneously. Starting power for the JFS is provided by a hydraulic motor driven by either of two hydraulic accumulators. The JFS shuts down automatically when the second engine reaches 50% rpm. The JFS may be used in-flight to perform a JFS assisted airstart.

The electrical power system consists of the two ac generators, two (three in the F-15E) transformer-rectifiers, an emergency ac/dc generator and a power distribution system. The JFS can provide sufficient RPM to the IDGs to power part of the electrical system. External electrical power may be connected to the aircraft through a receptacle near the nose gear well.

The two ac generators that are the primary source of electrical power are connected for split bus, non-synchronized, operation that enables them to supply different buses during normal operations, or for a single generator to supply both buses if one generator should fail. Current limiters are provided to prevent a fault in one generator system from shutting down both generators. Either generator is capable of supplying power to the entire system except for external ECM pods, which will be switched off-line. A utility hydraulic motor-driven emergency ac/dc generator provides power to a separate emergency power bus. If both main generators are inoperative, or both transformer-rectifiers fail, or some other combination of faults render the primary system inoperative, the emergency generator automatically comes on-line.

Three independent hydraulic systems are each pressurized to 3,000 psi by four Abex AMAD driven pumps. Reservoir level sensing is employed in all three systems for the purpose of isolating a leak. When a leak develops in a circuit, a valve senses the reservoir level and shuts off the affected circuit.

MISCELLANEOUS SYSTEMS

The F-15 uses two totally independent flight control systems. One is a traditional mechanical linkage to the hydraulic actuators at each control surface and serves as a backup system. The primary system is a triple redundant fly-by-wire (FBW) electronic system, the first incorporated on an American fighter. The mechanical and FBW systems normally work together, but either system alone is capable of providing sufficient aircraft control for flight. Spring cartridges provide simulated aerodynamic forces to the control stick and rudder pedals. The spring cartridges have trim actuators which actually move the neutral positions and thus the control surfaces. Lateral stick motion positions the ailerons, rudders, and stabilators to provide roll control. The ratio of aileron/differential stabilator deflection is adjusted automatically for different airspeeds. At subsonic speeds the roll ratio is high, and at supersonic speeds the ratio is reduced. The FBW control system is somewhat adaptive, and is able to compensate for damaged or missing control surfaces.

Jay Miller/Aerofax, Inc.

A two-seat F-15D-33-MC (82-0047) from the 33rd TFW at Eglin AFB shows the standard cross-country configuration of a centerline 610 gal. tank and a travel pod on each wing. Air intake is rotated forward in its usual approach position.

A Garrett environmental control system (ECS) provides conditioned air and pressurization for the cockpit and avionics, windshield anti-fog and anti-ice, the pilot's anti-g suit, and the canopy seal. Inlet air temperatures to avionics equipment are controlled to 82.5 ± 2.5° F at altitudes below 35,000 ft. (to minimize condensation when operating in high ambient humidities), and to 53 ± 3° F above 35,000 ft. The cooling capacity of the system is approximately 150,000 BTUs per hour.

The wiring system used on the F-15 was a major advance in miniaturization. As an example, a 22 lb. 0.772 sq. in. bundle used on the F-4 was miniaturized to a 9.6 lb. bundle with a cross section of 0.224 sq. in. There are approximately 19 miles of wiring onboard the aircraft.

External lighting includes six green electroluminescent formation lights. One is on each wingtip behind the position light, one on each side of the fuselage just forward of the cockpit, and one on each side of the fuselage just aft of the wing trailing edge. Position lights include a green light on the forward edge of the right wingtip, a red light on the forward edge of the left wingtip, and a white light just below the tip of the left vertical tail. There are three red anti-collision lights, one on the leading edge of each wing just outboard of the air intake, and another just below the tip of the right vertical tail fin. Taxi and landing lights are located on the nose gear strut.

AVIONICS

The Hughes Aircraft AN/APG-63 (AN/APG-70 in MSIP-II F-15C/D aircraft) radar set is a high frequency, pulse-Doppler attack radar designed primarily for air-to-air combat. The radar provides target range, range rate, antenna angles, and angular rates to the central computer for the computation of weapon attack mode parameters. Radar video is synthetically produced on the VSD (vertical situation display) located in the upper left of the pilot's instrument panel. The display is presented in symbol format, meaning it does not display actual targets but rather a computer derived "scene". The radar set consists of several line replaceable units and connecting waveguide assemblies, most of which are mounted inside the radome or in the forward left equipment bay.

The unit provides long-range detection and tracking of small, high-speed targets operating at all altitudes down to tree-top level. Since late-1979, aircraft have been fitted with a programmable signal processor (PSP), which provides the system with the ability to respond quickly to new tactics or to accommodate improved modes and weapons through software programming rather than by extensive hardware retrofit. The AN/APG-63 is the first U.S. airborne radar to incorporate a PSP. A radar ECCM (electronic counter countermeasure) feature provides the capability of detecting the presence and location of ECM devices. Special circuits automatically configure the radar for optimum search, acquisition and track performance against repeater and noise jamming devices.

The AN/APG-63 has a nominal 100 mile range, but is optimized for short and medium range combat. It employs a gridded traveling wave tube transmitter, digital Doppler signal processing, and digital mode/data management. These features enable the radar to operate over a wide range of pulse repetition frequencies (PRF), pulse widths and processing modes. The antenna is a planar array type, gimbaled in all three axes to maintain lock during air combat maneuvering. The ability of Hughes to provide a wide variety of PRFs in one unit was the primary consideration in winning the F-15 radar contract. The radar can operate in the following modes:

- The **long range search** (LRS) pulse-Doppler mode is the primary air-to-air surveillance mode. In this mode the radar operates in both high and medium pulse repetition frequencies (PRF). The pilot can select search ranges from 10 NM to 160 NM. The radar detection range performance is highly sensitive to the target cross sectional area, target Doppler conditions, ground clutter signal strength and tactical conditions (look-up versus look-down). The mixing of PRFs maximizes the potential for target detection for both tail aspect and nose aspect targets.
- The **velocity search** (VS) mode is a pulse-Doppler, long range surveillance mode in which the search display is presented in terms of target relative ground speed versus azimuth. This mode uses the high PRF waveform exclusively. It is used to provide early detection of reported targets in the long range, high closure rate, head-on aspect environment.
- The **short range search** (SRS) pulse-Doppler mode is optimized for a short range, high maneuvering air-to-air attack using AIM-9 missiles or the internal cannon. This mode uses the medium PRF and features displays selectable for 10, 20, and 40 NM scales. The medium PRF provides a better capability to break-out targets in a multi-target environment, and also provides improved range resolution.
- The **pulse** mode is a low PRF, non-Doppler mode provided as a back-up search and track capability in non-cluttered (look-up) conditions with no capability in look-down situations since no clutter rejection features are provided.
- In **beacon** mode the radar interrogates an airborne beacon (IFF/SIF) transponder. The beacon reply is displayed on the VSD as a coded target return. When the beacon mode is selected, the antenna roll gimbal is rotated 90° to provide the horizontal polarization required for beacon operation.
- The **manual track** mode is utilized when target tracking is inhibited due to problems in the radar tracking system.
- The **sniff** mode is a passive/active mode used to detect jamming of the radar channels or to provide a minimum of radar radiation time to prevent detection. This mode is gaining acceptance as an effective method of searching without giving away the current position of the F-15 by continuously broadcasting radar energy.

The AN/APG-70 is an extensively modified AN/APG-63, but utilizes the same antenna assembly and power supplies. Features of the modified transmitter includer higher average power and increased stability with better dynamic range. The redesigned receiver/exciter has increased bandwidth, improved tracking in ECCM mode, greater sensitivity, and longer detection ranges. A synthetic aperture radar (SAR) mode is incorporated in the version installed in the dual-mode F-15E, but not in the MSIP-II F-15C/D. SAR allows the detection of tank-sized

Jim Rotramel

One of three high-visibility markings tested at Luke during early-1976 was this red and white striped **F-15A-9-MC (73-103)**. The stripes were also applied to the top and bottom of the wings. Another F-15 (73-122) had black and white stripes, while the third (73-100) had broad yellow bands with black trim. None were approved for continued use.

Mick Roth

Four different versions of the Ferris "attitude deceptive" paint scheme were tried at Luke during mid-1976 including this **F-15A-11-MC (74-110)**. All four aircraft featured a false canopy under the forward fuselage. This scheme proved unsuccessful. The lack of national insignia and other markings, other than serial number, is noteworthy.

Jay Miller/Aerofax, Inc.

A good example of the "Compass Ghost" paint scheme used by all operational F-15s (except the F-15E) is presented by this **F-15A-16-MC (76-0076)** assigned to the 405th TTW at Luke. F-15s operated by Israel, Saudi Arabia, and Japan also use this paint scheme. This aircraft shows the current version of the national insignia on the forward fuselage.

A Japanese Air Self Defense Force F-15J (66-8825) retracts its landing gear immediately after take off. The position of the air intake and landing gear doors are noteworthy. "Compass Ghost" scheme is identical to USAF aircraft. JASDF aircraft have harmonic balancers on both vertical stabilizer tips and no ECM antennas under the forward fuselage.

Rarely seen unsensored view of Israeli Air Force ("Heyl Ha'Avir") F-15A "669". The aircraft is fully armed with no less than four AIM-9L "Sidewinders" and four AIM-7F "Sparrows". Centerline drop tank is standard. Unadulterated unit marking on vertical fin is noteworthy and rarely seen. This aircraft bears no visible kill markings on this side of nose.

Well-lit cockpit of F-15C. Windscreen bow serves as mounting point for three rear-view mirrors and small magnetic compass. Analog instrumentation is noteworthy.

Front cockpit of F-15E, 86-0183. Panel is absolutely state-of-the-art with heavy emphasis on CRT-type displays and digitized presentations. Note Raster-type HUD.

targets at ranges in excess of 30 miles and targets separated by 10 ft. can be distinguished individually. The radar also incorporates a "ground moving target detection" mode to assist the crew in finding ground-based vehicles. The SAR imagery is unaffected by adverse weather, smoke, haze, or fog.

A General Electric automatic flight control system (AFCS) provides for control augmentation, pitch/roll attitude hold, and altitude hold. Two separate AN/ARC-164 UHF radios are provided, both equipped with KY-58 (KY-28 in F-15A/B and non-MSIP F-15C/D) speech security units (scramblers). Both transmitter-receivers operate on manually selected frequencies, or on 20 preset frequency channels within the 225.000 to 399.975 MHz range. F-15Es and late F-15C/Ds (and those processed under the MSIP-II program) incorporate a "Have Quick" jam-resistant frequency-hopping radio.

IBM manufactures the high-speed, stored program, general purpose central computer. F-15As and F-15Cs before the MSIP-II program had central computers fitted with 32k of memory. MSIP-II increased this to 128k and tripled the speed of the processor. The computer provides air-to-air and air-to-ground steering and weapons delivery, navigation, flight director, and control and display management functions. It also provides the pilot with steering and weapon delivery dues, target data, avionic system status, and weapons configuration. A separate air data computer receives inputs from the pitot-static system, the angle of attack probes, the left total temperature probe, the altimeter setting knob, the nose landing gear door switch, and the flap switch. The computer then corrects these inputs for sensor error as required, computes various parameters from this data, and furnishes required parameters to the central computer. A Hazeltine AN/APX-76 IFF/SIF system is provided. This interrogator supports mode 1, mode 2, mode 3/A, mode 4, and mode C. Modes 1, 2, and 3/A are selective identification feature (SIF) modes, mode 4 is used for high confidence identification (crypto), and mode C is used for ATC altitude reporting.

The instrument landing system provides the capability for the aircraft to make a precision landing approach and descent. The radios and IFF controls are mounted in a stack directly in front of the pilot, just below the top of the instrument panel glare shield, as opposed to the more traditional location in one of the consoles. A self-contained Litton AN/ASN-109 inertial navigation system provides continuous present position monitoring and the capability for visual, TACAN, or radar updating in all aircraft except the F-15E.

The F-15E contains a self-contained, fully automatic, ring laser gyro (RLG) inertial navigation system (INS) which supplies the primary attitude reference for the aircraft and provides continuous present position monitoring. In addition, the INS provides aircraft attitude,

heading, velocity, and acceleration information to the LANTIRN, radar, and AFCS. The RLG is a rate-integrating gyro which does not use a spinning mass like a conventional gyroscope. The RLG detects and measures angular rotation by measuring the effective frequency difference between two contrarotating (one clockwise, one counterclockwise) laser beams in a ceramic block. As the two laser beams travel simultaneously around the cavity, mirrors reflect each beam around the enclosed path. When the gyro is at rest, the two beams have the same frequency because the optical path is the same in both directions. However, when the gyro is subjected to an angular turning rate about an axis perpendicular to the plane of the two beams, one beam sees a greater path length and the other sees a shorter path length. The two resonant frequencies change to adjust to the longer or shorter optical path, with the frequency differential being directly proportional to the angular turning rate.

EW SYSTEMS

The F-15's electronic warfare equipment is collectively known as TEWS (Tactical Electronic Warfare System). This system consists of the AN/ALR-56 radar warning receiver (RWR), the AN/ALQ-128 electronic warfare warning system (EWWS), AN/ALQ-135 internal countermeasures set (ICS or ICMS), AN/ALE-45 expendable countermeasures set (ECS or CMD), and the AN/ALQ-119 ECM pod. Apparent problems with systems development and integration caused F-15A/Bs to be deployed without the majority of the system installed, although most aircraft now have been retrofitted. The AN/ALR-56 RWR and AN/ALQ-128 EWWS were installed by TCTO 1F-15A-700 dated December 10, 1976, and the AN/ALQ-135(V) ICS was installed by TCTO 1F-15A-807 dated September 5, 1977, although it took several years to actually incorporate the systems in all operational aircraft. The two-seat F-15B/D aircraft are not fitted with the AN/ALQ-135 since the second seat occupies the area normally used by the system electronics. The two-seat F-15E has a redesigned forward fuselage that allows all components of TEWS to be carried, although integration problems with the AN/ALQ-135B are threatening to delay the aircraft's initial operational date.

AN/ALQ-119(V)—Westinghouse ECM pod family developed under QRC-335/522 beginning during 1970. These are dual-mode (deception-noise) jamming pods that operate in the E-band through J-band frequency range. The pod carried on the two-seat F-15B/Ds differs somewhat in having extended frequency coverage from the single-seat pod to minimize the effects of the two-seaters not carrying the AN/ALQ-135 system. The pod is being replaced by the AN/ALQ-131 pod in most applications. Also used by Israel and Japan on their F-15s. The

AN/ALQ-119(V) pod also is known as the "TEWS pod" when used on the F-15, and is carried on the centerline stores station (#5) after inclusion of TCTO 1F-15A-652 dated February 16, 1977. The pod also may be carried on either inboard wing stations (#2 or #8), but can not be operated since no wiring provisions were incorporated in the aircraft.

AN/ALQ-125(V)—Litton-Amecom direction finder set (DFS) electronic reconnaissance sensor (TEREC). The DFS provides a means of detecting, identifying, and locating enemy emitters near the battlefield. Emitter parameters are programmed into the system on a priority basis using the flight line test set AN/ALM-152. The system, as installed on the RF-4C, contains a fair number of cockpit displays and controls, and it is unknown where these are mounted in the F-15, although it is assumed a two-seat aircraft is used. The system establishes and maintains the hostile electronic order of battle in a tactical area, and provides rapid threat recognition and location, and in the case of the pod mounted F-15 system, data links this information to a field commander. Although listed in some documentation, it is unclear if the pod mounted system ever entered production, and it is possible that it never progressed beyond the prototype stage.

AN/ALQ-128—Magnavox electronic warfare warning system (EWWS). Antennas for the system are located in the nose radome, as well as the pod on top of the left vertical stabilizer. Warning coverage is different from the AN/ALR-56, but actual functions and capabilities are classified.

AN/ALQ-131(V)—Microprocessor controlled dual-mode (deception-noise) pod manufactured by Westinghouse/Loral. The AN/ALQ-131 pod employs variations of noise, transponder, and repeater techniques to counter SAM radars, AAA and AI fire control system radars, and velocity gate tracking radars. Developed as QRC-559 beginning during 1971, this system received a significant update under a $15.5 million "Have Exit" contract during August 1980. The block-II pods, which began qualification testing during November 1985, incorporate new hardware as well as new deception techniques. Block-I pods are also used by Israel and Japan on their F-15s. The pod is of modular construction and, depending on the exact mission, can vary from 85 to 154 in. long. Other dimensions are 12 in. wide, 25 in. high while weight is between 100 and 150 lbs., depending on exact configuration.

AN/ALQ-135—Northrop manufactured internal countermeasures set (ICS). The function of the ICS is to counter surface-to-air missile, airborne interceptor, and anti-aircraft artillery attacks using active jamming with a minimum of pilot activity. Early sets contain two bands, with band-1 covering E-band through G-band, and band-2 operating in G-band through I-band, with a frequency overlap in G-band. Later units use three bands, with band-1 operating in E-band through G-band, band 2 covering G-band and H-band, and band-3 operating in H-band through J-band. The system is composed of six line replaceable units (LRU) plus waveguides and antennas. Three of the LRUs are control oscillators, and three are amplifiers. Initial development commenced during August 1974, with production beginning during September 1975. An improved version, the AN/ALQ-135B is used by the F-15C and F-15E. More than 1,000 sets, worth more than $2 billion, had been produced through the end of 1986, and during February 1987, Northrop received a $333 million contract to begin production of Lot III for the F-15E. The system uses three small antennas located under the forward fuselage, with additional antennas carried on the back of the fuselage boom-extensions, one on the right of the F-15C and one on each side of the F-15E. Some (but not all) Israeli aircraft also carry these antenna, indicating that they probably carry the AN/ALQ-135 system. Since the majority of the electronics is carried in the area occupied by the second seat in the F-15B/D, the AN/ALQ-135 has been deleted from these two-seat aircraft. The F-15E has a redesigned forward fuselage and ammunition feed system that enabled it to become the first two-seater to carry the AN/ALQ-135B, although during May 1989 the AF admitted to having problems integrating the system into the aircraft.

AN/ALQ-153—Tail warning set produced by Westinghouse. This is a rear-looking pulse-Doppler radar that detects and discriminates approaching missiles and aircraft. It is a range-gated system that will possibly interface with the TEWS. Development tests were completed during 1976. First two operational units delivered during April 1980 for installation on a B-52. Some documentation lists a possible application to the F-15E, although this

An F-15D-35-MC (83-0047) shows the lack of AN/ALQ-135 antennas under its nose. The second seat occupies the area used by the ECM electronics in the single-seater. The F-15E is the first two-seater to incorporate AN/ALQ-135.

This F-15C-38-MC (84-0018) assigned to the Munitions Division (3247th TS/3246th TW) has an AIM-120A AMRAAM on the left pylon outboard rail. Kill marking on nose and video cameras under wingtip and aft fuselage are noteworthy.

has yet to be officially confirmed.

AN/ALQ-184—Manufactured by Raytheon, this is a major update to the AN/ALQ-119 pod. Improvements include higher radiated power, enhanced ECM techniques, improved reliability and easier maintenance. The antennas are of a new multi-beam design. This pod is being procured along with block-II versions of the AN/ALQ-131 as the standard AF replacement for the AN/ALQ-119(V).

AN/ALR-56—Radar warning receiver designed and manufactured by Loral. Receives, analyses, and stores threat data transmitted by surface-to-air missile radars, air intercept radars, anti-artillery control and communications systems. This data is provided to the pilot as warning lights, CRT displays, and audible warnings. The RWR also provides automated control and tuning data for the AN/ALQ-135 system and AN/ALE-45 dispenser set. Determination of jamming requirements is made by comparison of received signals with a stored program threat table. The set is composed of a processor, low-band receiver, high-band-receiver, countermeasures display, receiver controller, power supply, and antenna system. The solid-state, digitally controlled, dual-channel receivers cover roughly C-band through J-band. The antenna system consists of four circularly polarized spiral high-band antenna assemblies, each within its own radome (one on the trailing edge of each tail, and one on the leading edge of each wingtip), and a small low-band blade antenna on the front nose gear door.

A major update is the AN/ALR-56C with a significantly faster processor capable of handling more threats and greater signal densities. Principle functions are: programmed signal search; signal acquisition and analysis; establishing threat priorities; jammer management; passive countermeasure management; and providing visual and audible alerts. The AN/ALR-56C is fitted to all F-15C/D aircraft, and a December 1986 contract for $39 million provided 42 sets for initial F-15E production.

AN/ALE-45—Tracor-manufactured expendable countermeasure dispenser set. The AN/ALE-45 is a solid-state microprocessor controlled dispenser which interfaces to AN/ALR-56 for automatic operation. The set determines the best dispensing program based on operating mode, payload management inputs, available expendables, threat type, altitude, velocity, and aspect angle to the threat. The set can also be controlled manually by the pilot. The dispensing program is incorporated into replaceable modules that can be changed on the flight-line. The set has four dispensers, each with two magazines, and is capable of dispensing chaff, flares, and expendable jammers. Two dispensers are located in the bottom of the fuselage immediately forward of each main landing gear wheel well, although the system is seldom seen fitted while the aircraft are in the United States. Installation provisions exist in all F-15C/Ds, and the F-15E, but apparently not in AF F-15A/Bs, although it is probably used by Israeli F-15As. At least some part of the wiring was incorporated into AF F-15As, and the system control switch exists on the throttle quadrant of all F-15s.

FOREIGN EW SYSTEMS

AL/L-8202 (Israel)—ECM pod manufactured by the Elta Electronics Industries, Ltd. subsidiary of Israeli Aircraft Industries (IAI), Ltd. The pod is designed to provide self-protection against both surface and airborne threats. It has wide frequency coverage (F-band through J-band), and a high broadband output with selectable ECM techniques. Antennas are located at both ends of the pod, which is 114 in. long, 10 in. wide, 15 in. high, and weighs 90 lbs. The pod is used by all Israeli variants of the F-15, as well as most other Heyl Ha' Avir aircraft.

J/ALQ-8 (Japan)—Indigenously designed and produced self-defense system roughly similar in capabilities to the AF/Northrop AN/ALQ-135.

J/APR-4 (Japan)—Radar warning receiver set designed and manufactured by Tokyo Keiki. The system was heavily based on the experience gained during the development of the J/APR-2 for the McDonnell/Mitsubishi F-4EJ and the J/APR-3 for the Mitsubishi F-1. The system is functionally similar to, but less sophisticated than, the AF/Loral AN/ALR-56, and is capable of processing multiple inputs simultaneously in a dense electromagnetic environment. Utilizes a digital computer with a reprogrammable software package to permit rapid reconfiguration. The cockpit display is similar in size, shape, and location to the TEWS display in USAF F-15s. The display provides for multiple threat data presentations in alphanumeric and graphic formats. The system interfaces with the J/ALQ-8 for coordination of defensive countermeasures.

The first F-15E-41-MC (86-0183) carried unique markings on the forward fuselage and vertical stabilizers. This aircraft featured all new F-15E systems but did not have the modified aft fuselage found on later F-15Es.

Early F-15Es (like 87-0169) were assigned to the 461st TFTS/405th TFTW at Luke AFB for training purposes. Note the exaggerated hardpoints that allow drag-reducing tangential carriage on the type-4 CFTs.

ARMAMENT:

Fixed armament consists of one General Electric M61A1 20mm Vulcan rotary cannon in the shoulder area of the right wing root. The muzzle is positioned well aft of the main engine air intake to prevent ingestion of exhaust gases. The cannon has six barrels, weighs 275 lbs., is electrically controlled, hydraulically driven, and has a muzzle velocity of 3,380 ft. per second. The gun has selectable firing rates of 4,000 or 6,000 rounds per minute. A total of 940 rounds of ammunition are carried by all variants except the F-15E. A drum assembly provides storage for the 20mm ammunition, and is directly linked to the ammunition conveyer system and the return conveyer system. An exit unit removes ammunition from the drum and an entrance unit returns spent cases, misfired rounds and cleared rounds to the drum. The complete ammunition cycle forms a closed loop from the ammunition drum to the gun and return.

The components that make up a complete round or cartridge used in the M61A1 gun are: a brass or steel cartridge case, an electric primer, propellant powder, and the projectile. The complete cartridge is approximately 6.625 in. long and weighs roughly 1/2 lb. Three types of ammunition currently are available. The 20mm target cartridge (TP) is ball ammunition with a hollow projectile that does not contain filler. The 20mm armor piercing incendiary (API) projectile is charged with an incendiary composition that ignites on impact. And the 20mm high explosive incendiary (HEI) cartridge explodes with an incendiary effect after it has penetrated the target. The HEI cartridge is normally used against aircraft and light ground targets.

In order to gain additional space for electronic equipment (primarily the AN/ALQ-135 set), the F-15E has a redesigned ammunition handling system that uses a linkless feed system. The ammunition capacity was initially stated as 512 rounds, but ever increasing need for volume for the electronics has reduced this to the vicinity of 450 rounds in current production aircraft. The new system required the use of a small fairing on the underside of the fuselage directly beneath the ammunition drum, and this is one of the identifying features of the F-15E.

The basic F-15 is equipped with nine numbered external stores stations: The left outboard wing station is #1; the left inboard wing station is #2, the left forward fuselage missile station is #3 while the left aft fuselage missile station is #4; the centerline is #5; the right fuselage missile stations are #6 (forward) and #7 (aft); the right inboard wing station is #8; and the right outboard wing station is #9. The inboard wing station pylons are both equipped with two rail launchers for AIM-9/AIM-120

missiles, effectively giving four additional stations.

The air-superiority F-15 is capable of carrying a variety of air-to-air missiles including the AIM-7F/M *Sparrow III*, AIM-9J/L/P/M *Sidewinder*, and the AGM-120A AMRAAM. The AIM-7s are carried on the four fuselage missile stations. The AIM-9s are rail launched, and are carried mounted on either side of each inboard wing station weapons pylon. AIM-120As may replace any of the AIM-7s and/or AIM-9s, although there currently are some vibration/flutter problems when they are carried on the two forward fuselage stations. Each of the inboard wing stations and the centerline accommodate a variety of conventional and special stores carried singularly or on multiple ejector racks (MER). The MER-200 racks used on the F-15 are of a different design than earlier MERs, and are rated to 7.33 g as opposed to the usual 5 g.

Among the weapons approved for the F-15 to date are: Mk 20 *Rockeye*, Mk 82, Mk 84, BLU-27, CBU-52, CBU-58, and CBU-71 bombs; the Matra Durandal runway denial weapon; SUU-20 training weapons; ALQ-119(V) ECM pods; and Mk 57 and Mk 61 nuclear stores. Drop tanks containing 610 gals. may be carried on the three inboard stations of all F-15s. The outboard wing stations, rated at 1,300 lbs. each, are not currently cleared to carry any stores (according to the flight manual), although both ECM pods and HARM have been observed there on occasion. The maximum permissible external load for the F-15C/D is 23,600 lbs.

A partial listing of the F-15E's cleared stores, with the maximum allowed in parenthesis, includes: Mk 20 *Rockeye* (26), Mk 82 (26), Mk 84 (7), BSU-49 (26), BSU-50 (7), GBU-8 (5), GBU-10 (7), GBU-12 (15), GBU-15 (2), CBU-52 (25), CBU-58 (25), CBU-71 (25), CBU-87 (25), CBU-89 (25), CBU-90 (25), CBU-92 (25), CBU-93 (25) bombs; LAU-3A rockets (9); SUU-20 training weapons (5); U-33 tow target (1); AGM-65 *Mavericks* (6); AGM-120 (2); ALQ-119(V) ECM pods; and B61 nuclear stores (5). An AN/AXQ-14 data link pod is used in conjunction with the GBU-15 precision guided weapon, and is carried on the centerline station. LANTIRN navigation (AN/AAQ-13) and targeting (AN/AAQ-14) pods are carried on additional stations just aft of the lower edge of the air intakes, and a *Pave Tack* pod can be carried on the centerline station.

Additional weapons expected to be cleared for use on the F-15 include: AGM-45 *Shrike*; AGM-88 HARM; AGM-84 *Harpoon*; and the new ASRAAM missile. A close support weapon being developed by General Electric will likely also be cleared for use on the F-15E. This GEPOD 30mm cannon can be carried on the inboard pylons and the centerline. The pod contains a four-barrel GE430 cannon with 350 rounds of the same depleted-uranium ammunition developed for the A-10's GAU-8. The rate of fire

F-15E-43-MC (87-0178) is assigned to the 4th TFW CO. Multi-colored stripe represents all 4th TFW squadrons, though only the 336th TFS is currently F-15E equipped.

This F-15E-42-MC (86-0187) of the 461st TFTS is shown without the type-4 CFTs. Stripe on tail is black with yellow highlights. Lack of unit badge on intake is noteworthy.

Four "Eagles", including 73-111, were painted in the Ferris "attitude deceptive" paint scheme at Luke AFB. Wing Commander's multi-color stripes are visible on fin tip.

The second prototype F-15A (71-281) was used for a short time by the NASA Dryden Flight Research Center. Aircraft was painted gloss white with a royal blue stripe.

A bottom view of one of the Ferris painted F-15s clearly shows the "false canopy" on the forward fuselage. Paint is flaking off around engine compartment due to heat.

is 2,400 rounds per minute and the effective range exceeds 7,000 ft.

F-15C/D/Es are capable of carrying conformal fuel tanks (CFT), and these provide additional weapons stations. Originally called FAST-packs (Fuel and Sensor Tactical), the low-drag CFTs contain approximately 114 cubic ft. of usable volume. They attach to the outer side of each engine intake, under the wing root, and are designed to the same load factors as the basic F-15 (i.e., 9 g). The CFTs can be installed or removed in 15 mins. At subsonic and transonic speeds the CFTs actually improve the aircraft's drag coefficient (being slightly area-ruled), and impose a minimal penalty at supersonic speeds. In theory the CFTs can be configured to include a variety of systems, such as reconnaissance sensors, laser designators, radar detection and jamming equipment, in addition to 750 gals. of fuel. All external stores stations remain available with the CFTs in place, and McDonnell Douglas has developed a new weapons attachment system which can extend the operating radius with large external loads by up to 40%. Known as tangential carriage, it involves the installation of six stations in two rows of stub pylons on the lower corner and bottom of each type-4 CFT. Each of these stations is capable of carrying 2,000 lbs., and four of them are wired to support AIM-7 or AIM-120A missiles. The use of tangential carriage greatly reduces the drag associated with carrying external stores when compared to the normal MERs. Early type-1 CFTs have attach points for four Sparrows or one MER, and are used primarily on F-15C/Ds instead of the F-15E.

The AN/ASQ-T11 and AN/ASQ-T13 air combat maneuvering instrumentation system (ACMI) pods may also be carried. The pod is the airborne portion of an ACMI training system, and contains a data link system that enables the ground to monitor the aircraft's fire control system and flight instrumentation during air combat maneuvering training. The pod is the same general size and shape as an AIM-9 Sidewinder, and is suspended in the same manner as the AIM-9.

MXU-648/A cargo (personnel) pods may be carried on the inboard wing pylons and/or the centerline station. The pod is a converted BLU-27 fire bomb shell. The empty weight of the pod is 125 lbs., and a maximum of 300 lbs. may be loaded.

POWERPLANTS:

During December 1967, the AF and Navy agreed to conduct a joint engine development program for the F-14B and F-X. Their goal was to develop a high-performance afterburning turbofan Advanced Technology Engine (ATE, also called the Advanced Turbine Engine Gas Generator [ATEGG] program), drawing upon experience gained from the development of the lift-cruise engine of the still-born U.S.-West German V/STOL, the AMSA bomber program, and several demonstrator engine programs of the 1960s. The proposed new engine was required to produce 40% more thrust and weigh 25% less than the 12-year old TF30 used in the F-111. New lightweight materials and improved design promised more efficient compressor stage-loading and higher turbine temperatures. The new engine was to generate more than 20,000 lbs. of thrust and have a 9:1 thrust-to-weight ratio.

On April 8, 1968, RFPs were sent to General Electric (GE), Pratt & Whitney (P&W) and the Allison Division of General Motors. At the end of August, OSD authorized the award of two 18-month contracts totalling $117.45 million to GE and P&W. The competition was won by Pratt & Whitney on March 27, 1970, with the initial award, valued at $448,200,000 covering development, testing,

and procurement of 90 engines. The AF and Navy had several significant disagreements concerning the management and procurement structures associated with the ATE program. It ended up with a Joint Engine Program Office (JEPO) being formed which later was absorbed into the F-15 SPO, with matrix reporting from Brig.Gen. Bellis to the Chief of the Naval Materiel Command on matters concerning the Navy engine version.

The advanced afterburning turbofan was developed largely from the P&W JTF16 demonstrator engine of the mid-1960s. The AF version was to have less thrust but a longer interval between overhauls because of the more stringent Navy emergency thrust requirements during carrier landings. The AF F100-PW-100 engine was to use the same gas generator section (core engine) as the Navy F401-PW-400, but the size of the fan (and hence total mass flow and bypass ratio), afterburner, nozzle, and other significant components were not common.

P&W had to adhere to two major technical milestones: the preliminary flight rating test (PFRT), which was completed during February 1972; and the final qualification test, which was completed under controversy during May 1973. The first milestone cleared the engine for use during flight tests, while the second demonstrated its suitability for operational use. The F100 final qualification test was the only milestone the F-15 program failed to meet on time, the original schedule calling for test completion during February 1973. During this test, the F100 was supposed to run for 150 hours at various simulated altitudes and Mach numbers, but during February 1973, seven months after the F-15 had started flying, the test engine threw a fan blade which destroyed the fan section.

Nevertheless, during March the AF approved the production of initial F100s conditional on meeting the 150 hour milestone by May 1973. In an attempt to ensure P&W would meet the May date, Bellis deferred the high-

Mach and high-altitude portions of the endurance test. Since it was not envisioned that the F-15 would ever actually operate at high Mach numbers, or at high altitude, this was an extremely practical decision, and Pratt & Whitney did complete the revised test during May. However, the commotion the decision caused within Congress, and among critics of the F-15, very nearly caused the entire F-15 program to be cancelled. The engine eventually passed the complete, unmodified, endurance test on October 12, 1973. The cause of the original failure was traced to a minor manufacturing defect in the prototype engine, plus some undetected rust contamination in the test chamber that had flaked off the walls to be ingested internally. The engine would, however, continue to be a source of F-15 and, eventually F-16, problems.

During November 1970, because of F-14 funding cuts, the Navy pared its engine request from 179 to 69 units. Since the larger number of engines set the original cost, this cut required a new formula with a higher price per engine for the AF. During the spring of 1971, the Navy cut further its order to 58 engines to fit the lagging F-14B development effort. An even more significant problem shared by both the F-15 and the F-14 programs arose during June 1971 when Pratt & Whitney disclosed an unexpected rise in FY73 program costs. The total cost of development then was expected to be $63 million higher than first estimated, due in part to technical problems with the Navy version, additional testing requirements, inflation, and a decline in P&W's business base. Under the terms of the contract, P&W was to absorb 10% of the overrun, with the Navy and AF each responsible for 45%.

During June 1971, P&W wrote a letter to the JEPO asking that the F100/F401 program be granted use of a B-45 engine testbed that had been used on numerous previous engine projgects by both P&W and GE. The JEPO responded that the B-45 program would prove to be too expensive, and rejected the request (it is interesting to note that the proposed test program would have concentrated on the area of the flight envelope that has proven to be the F100's achilles heel).

The engine difficulties and the attendant cost overrun announced during June 1971 were the result of a decision to drop the design of the primary aerodynamic compressor system installed in the first F100 engines and replace it with a more advanced design. Both had been carried from the start of the program as potential production units, but the advanced version added about 100 lbs. to the weight of the engine. It thus had been set aside due to the Navy's F401 stringent weight requirements. Inferior operating performance with the primary compressor was discovered during the fall of 1970, and by the summer of 1971 the decision in favor of the advanced version had been made. The switch, which caused an approximately four month delay in the program, was no doubt a factor in the Navy's decision to cancel its F401 production contract. Because of tight scheduling, the engines in the first five F-15 test aircraft (71-280/284) were the so-called Series-I (YF 100) powerplants, which used the 1st generation aerodynamic compressor. The first Series-II (F100) engine with the advanced compressor ran in a testbed during the spring of 1972 and all later F-15s were fitted with engines incorporating it.

Early F-15s use two Pratt & Whitney (a division of United Technologies) F100-PW-100 turbofans, each rated at 23,830 lbs. thrust with afterburner. Since all accessories (generators, etc.) are mounted in the AMAD, the left and right engines of the F-15 are interchangeable, simplifying maintenance considerably.

The F100 is a two-shaft turbofan with a high-augmentation afterburner. The engine is equipped with a direct pitot-type titanium intake with a fixed nose bullet. There are 21 inlet guide vanes in a single row equipped with variable-camber trailing edges. The fan has three stages and the fan blades and discs are of titanium construction. The compressor is a ten-stage axial design constructed primarily of titanium, Inconel, and other high-temperature alloys. The first three stages of the compressor are equipped with variable stator blades to allow optimum airflow scheduling. The annular combustion chamber is fabricated of Haynes-188 cobalt based alloy with film cooling. It is equipped with dual fuel injectors and a capacitor-discharge ignition system, each containing an independent engine mounted generator and three igniter plugs, two for the engine and one for the afterburner. The F100 is designed to be smokeless, and this is achieved by concentrating combustion on the front of the burner, and using extremely high operating temperatures. The high pressure turbine has two stages

Former spin-test prototype (71-287) was also bailed to Dryden FRC, and has flown in numerous engine and flight control test programs under NASA sponsorship. Aircraft was painted overall gloss white with flat black anti-glare shield.

NASA's 71-287 was used to test the new Digital Electronic Engine Controller (DEEC) that would be included on the F100-PW-220 engine version used in later F-15s. An extra pitot tube is visible just ahead of forward UHF antenna.

During the summer of 1983, 71-287 was used for demonstrations of the Engine Model Derivative (EMD) program which proved the value of the F100-PW-229. Space Shuttle thermal protection system materials were tested on right wing.

Ames Research Center (which now operates Dryden) has recently assigned 71-287 a new NASA number (835). Aircraft continues to be based at Dryden and supports numerous NASA programs. Note "F-15 HIDEC" markings on fuselage.

One of the Category II F-15As (72-116/117/118 or 120) that was sold to Israel at the conclusion of the test program. Note the prototype configuration fin-tip pods. Other photos show this aircraft to have the small speed brake.

35

McDonnell Douglas via Hughes

Israeli Air Force F-15A, "802" with rarely seen unsensored markings. Four Syrian Air Force kills are readily discernible on nose, just ahead of and below the windscreen.

Katsuhiko Tokunaga

Japanese F-15DJs are essentially identical to their F-15D counterparts. Note the harmonic balancers instead of ECM pods on both vertical stabilizers. Japanese aircraft carry national insignia on the top and bottom of both wings.

with directionally solidified alloy blades. The low-pressure turbine has two stages with PWA-73 coated alloy blades and a maximum allowable speed of 10,400 rpm.

The afterburner has five concentric spray rings in flow from the core engine, and two slightly further downstream in the fan bypass airflow. The flameholder assembly is downstream of the spray rings, and is connected with a high-energy ignition system that permits a modulated light-up. The outer bypass duct and other major afterburner assemblies are fabricated in sheet and stringer titanium, while the interior liner is of coated Haynes-188.

The convergent-divergent axisymmetric exhaust nozzle is a multi-flap, balanced beam arrangement giving a wide range in area and profile. The nozzles are positioned pneumatically by engine bleed air. With the landing gear down and the engine in "IDLE", the nozzles will be approximately 80% open. With the landing gear up, the nozzle is at minimum area at all times except at "MIL" power or above. The nozzles are full open only when in full afterburner. In theory, 17 small titanium covers protect the actuators for the nozzles, but in service it is not uncommon to see these "turkey feathers" removed from the engines since they are a maintenance burden (and cost $1,200 each). The F100-PW-100 is 191.2 in. long, 46.5 in. in diameter, and weighs 3,033 lbs.

Beginning during October 1986, F-15s started being delivered with the improved F100-PW-220 version, which delivers 23,450 lbs. thrust with afterburner. Although it generates slightly less thrust, the new engine provides a small improvement in specific fuel economy, and generally increased reliability. Most earlier -100 engines have been modified to the newer -220 configuration in U.S. and foreign service. The F100-PW-220 is 208 in. long, 46.5 in. in diameter, weighs 3,184 lbs., and shares 81% of its parts and 90% of its GSE with the earlier engine. The engine's ignition system consists of four ig-

niters, two for the engine and two for the afterburner, as opposed to the three igniters of the F100-PW-100. The exhaust nozzles are not designed to be equipped with turkey feathers. Major improvements incorporated into the F100-PW-220 include:

- Increased core life—4,000 cycles (9 years) for the first inspection and an 8,000 cycle engine life expectancy. The use of single crystal 1st and 2nd stage turbine blades is a major contributor to this feature.
- Digital Electronic Engine Control (DEEC)—reduces control system complexity by replacing both the Engine Electronic Control (EEC) and the hydro-mechanical Unified Fuel Control (UFC) units employed on the F100-PW-100.
- Gear-type main fuel pump—400 fewer parts than the high-speed variable-vane pump. This pump doubles the life expectancy to 2,000 hours.
- Improved augmentor (afterburner) with better cooling and stronger materials.
- A light-off detector (LOD) that senses augmentor ignition and, with the DEEC, permits faster throttle transients. If the LOD does not sense a "light-off", it automatically retards the throttles to "MIL", terminates the fuel flow to the afterburner and checks all systems. If everything checks good, the LOD will automatically attempt two additional relights. If these attempts are unsuccessful, the LOD is disabled by the DEEC, and one additional relight is attempted, using tailpipe pressure to verify an afterburner light-off.

The F100-PW-220 incorporates an engine monitoring system which consists of the DEEC and an engine diagnostic unit (EDU). The DEEC and EDU continuously monitor electrical control components and engine operation to detect engine failures. Abnormal engine operation and either intermittent or hard failures of com-

ponents are detected and flagged for maintenance personnel. During abnormal engine operation or component failure, the EDU will record engine and aircraft data as an aid to maintenance troubleshooting. The EDU also maintains engine life-cycle information.

During early-1984, the AF announced that a second engine was being procured for all future F-15 and F-16 aircraft, and the Navy also selected the engine to power the F-14A(Plus) and F-14D. This engine is the General Electric F110-GE-100, which generates 27,600 lbs. of thrust with afterburner. The F110 is designed for modular assembly to facilitate maintenance and repair, and numerous borescope ports are positioned along the engine for inspecting critical areas, such as the compressor, combustor, and turbine assemblies. The core is basically a scaled-down version of the F101 that powers the B-1B coupled with a scaled-up version of the F404 (F/A-18A) fan assembly. The engine is 181.9 in. long, 46.5 in. in diameter, and weighs 3,300 lbs. It has identical attachment points and fittings to the F100-PW-220, and can be used interchangeably. An annual competition has been staged to determine the number of powerplants produced by each contractor, with General Electric winning a 50.4% share to date. Although there is no reason why they could not be, no GE engines have been used in the F-15 as of mid-1989.

The Improved Performance engine (IPE) program has produced engines from each manufacturer that have an increase to approximately 29,000 lbs. sea-level static thrust. These engines, the F100-PW-229 and F110-GE-129, have been successfully demonstrated in an F-16C and a modified F-15A. Both engines could eventually power the F-16C/D and F-15E. The engines are currently undergoing total accumulated cycle tests in which they have to successfully pass 4,000 cycles.

Air is fed to the engines by two straight two-dimensional external compression inlets, one on each side of the fuselage. Air inlet controllers are provied by Hamilton Standard, with actuators by National Water Lift. The inlets are identical, but completely separate, and are capable of operating asymmetrically. Each system consists of three variable ramps, a variable diffuser ramp, and a variable bypass door. The entire intake rotates about a pivot on the lower cowl lip to provide optimum airflow at all angles of attack. The upper leading edge can rotate up to 11° below and 4° above the horizontal. The variable ramps provide air at optimum subsonic flow to the face of the engine throughout the aircraft speed range. Ramp position is controlled by the air inlet controller, as is the bypass door. The bypass door controls the inlet duct Mach number by opening to automatically bypass excess air. The air inlet controller, one for each inlet, utilizes angle of attack, temperature, ramp actuator position, aircraft Mach number and inlet duct Mach number to schedule the ramps and bypass door operation. The first ramp is locked in the up position unless the aircraft is above 0.5 Mach. A series of tests in the AF Arnold Engineering Development Center wind tunnel has established that the inlet is essentially stall-free at any flight attitude and all altitudes. The inlets also provide a small measure of lift, and serve to unload the horizontal stabilator, much the same as a canard, allowing a smaller tail surface.

Internal fuel in the F-15A/B is carried in four Goodyear fuselage tanks and two wet-wing tanks with a total capacity of 1,759 gals. Block-10 and later aircraft incorporated ECP-253M4 and carry approximately 30 gals. (200 lbs.) more fuel in tank #1 for a total of 1,789 gals. Aircraft prior to block-10 were not retrofitted with the modification. The F-15C/D has six fuselage tanks and two wet-wing tanks for a total of 2,070 gals. The F-15E has four interconnected fuselage tanks and two wet-wing tanks, and carries 51 gals. less than the F-15C. Recommended fuel is JP-4 or JP-8, although the aircraft is capable of limited operations on commercial Jet-A. The internal wing tanks and fuselage tank number 1 are transfer tanks. The tanks are arranged so that fuel from all internal tanks will gravity transfer even if the transfer pumps fail. Regulated engine bleed air transfers fuel from the external tanks to any internal tank that will accept it, and also provides a positive pressure on all internal tanks. The fuel transfer system is completely automated. Engine feed tanks are self-sealing for protection from up to 0.50 caliber projectiles, and all internal tanks have reticulated foam for fire/explosion suppression. Wherever possible, fuel lines have been routed inside the fuel tanks, and wherever that was not possible, the lines are covered with a self-sealing material. Single point refueling is provided, and an in-flight refueling receptacle is mounted in the left wing root. The in-flight refueling receptacle incorporates pyrotechnic devices which can open a stuck slipway door to permit emergency refueling. The door can not then be closed in flight.

Optional conformal fuel tanks (CFT) attach to the sides of the F-15C/D/E's engine air intakes, beneath the wing, and contain 750 gals. each. Some F-15A/Bs in U.S. and Israeli service have been modified to carry the CFTs. Each CFT is pressurized by a self-contained ram air pressurization and vent system. The CFT fuel compartments incorporate explosion suppression foam slabs for enhanced survivability.

All internal, CFT and external fuel (except engine feed tanks) may be dumped overboard from an outlet at the trailing edge of the right wing tip. Provisions are provided for up to three 610 gal. drop tanks, one on the centerline, and one on each inboard wing station. External tanks built after January 1977 have improved lightning strike protection, and earlier tanks were modified by TCTO 1F-15A-659 dated February 16, 1977.

Mitsubishi produced F-15J is externally identical to the USAF F-15C, except for the lack of an ECM pod on the vertical stabilizer and missing ECM antennas under the forward fuselage. All Japanese F-15s are painted "Compass Ghost".

A Royal Saudi Air Force F-15D shows the standard markings for the type. Note the lack of an ECM pod on the vertical stabilizer. Most markings are duplicated in both Arabic and English. Aircraft is painted standard "Compass Ghost".

FOREIGN F-15 UNITS

Country	Wing	Squadron	Location	Dates
Japan	2nd	203rd	Chitose	Apr 83 - Pres.
		207th	Chitose	Apr 85 - Pres.
Japan	5th	202nd	Nyutabaru	Dec 82 - Pres.
		301st	Nyutabaru	Apr 87 - Pres.
Japan	7th	204th	Hyakuri	Apr 84 - Pres.
		305th	Hyakuri	Apr 86 - Pres.
Israel	---	133rd	???	Dec 76 - Pres.
		???		???
KSA	---	6th	Taif	Aug 81 - Pres.
		13th	Dhahran	???
		???	Khamis	???

PRODUCTION AIRCRAFT

Dash Number	Serial Number	# of Thru	a/c	Comments	Dash Number	Serial Number	# of Thru	a/c	Comments	Dash Number	Serial Number	# of Thru	a/c	Comments
F-15A-1-MC	71-280 – 71-281	2			F-15C-23-MC	78-0523 – 78-0550	28			F-15D-30-MC	81-0061 – 81-0062	2		
F-15A-2-MC	71-282 – 71-284	3			F-15D-21-MC	78-0561 – 78-0565	5			F-15D-31-MC	81-0063 – 81-0065	3		
F-15A-3-MC	71-285 – 71-286	2			F-15D-22-MC	78-0566 – 78-0570	5			F-15D-32-MC	81-0066	1		ex-USAF, converted to RSAF F-15D 81-0003
F-15A-4-MC	71-287 – 71-289	3			F-15D-23-MC	78-0571 – 78-0574	4							
F-15B-3-MC	71-290	1			F-15D-24-MC	79-0004 – 79-0006	3							
F-15B-4-MC	71-291	1			F-15D-25-MC	79-0007 – 79-0011	5			F-15DJ-32-MC	81-0068 – 81-0069	2		JASDF
F-15A-5-MC	72-113 – 72-115	3			F-15D-26-MC	79-0012 – 79-0014	3			F-15DJ-33-MC	81-0070 – 81-0071	2		JASDF
F-15A-5-MC	72-116	1		To Israel	F-15C-24-MC	79-0015 – 79-0037	23			F-15C-33-MC	82-0008 – 82-0022	15		
F-15A-6-MC	72-117 – 72-118	2		To Israel	F-15C-25-MC	79-0038 – 79-0058	21			F-15C-34-MC	82-0023 – 82-0038	16		
F-15A-6-MC	72-119	1		Streak Eagle	F-15C-26-MC	79-0059 – 79-0081	23			F-15D-33-MC	82-0044 – 82-0045	2		
F-15A-6-MC	72-120	1		To Israel	F-15J-24-MC	79-0280 – 79-0281	2		JASDF	F-15D-34-MC	82-0046 – 82-0048	3		
F-15A-7-MC	73-085 – 73-089	5			F-15DJ-26-MC	79-0282 – 79-0285	4		JASDF	F-15C-35-MC	83-0010 – 83-0034	25		
F-15A-8-MC	73-090 – 73-097	8			F-15DJ-29-MC	79-0286 – 79-0287	2		JASDF	F-15C-36-MC	83-0035 – 83-0043	9		
F-15A-9-MC	73-098 – 73-107	10			F-15C-27-MC	80-0002 – 80-0023	22			F-15D-35-MC	83-0046 – 83-0048	3		
F-15B-7-MC	73-108 – 73-110	3			F-15C-28-MC	80-0024 – 80-0038	15			F-15D-36-MC	83-0049 – 83-0050	2		
F-15B-8-MC	73-111 – 73-112	2			F-15C-29-MC	80-0039 – 80-0053	15			F-15DJ-36-MC	83-0052 – 83-0053	2		JASDF
F-15B-9-MC	73-113 – 73-114	2			F-15D-27-MC	80-0054 – 80-0055	2			F-15C-35-MC	83-0054 – 83-0055	2		Foreign Military Sales (Israel)
F-15A-10-MC	74-081 – 74-093	13			F-15D-28-MC	80-0056 – 80-0057	2							
F-15A-11-MC	74-094 – 74-111	18			F-15D-29-MC	80-0058 – 80-0061	4			F-15C-36-MC	83-0056 – 83-0062	7		Foreign Military Sales (Israel)
F-15A-12-MC	74-112 – 74-136	25			F-15C-28-MC	80-0062 – 80-0067	6		Royal Saudi AF					
F-15B-10-MC	74-137 – 74-138	2			F-15C-29-MC	80-0068 – 80-0074	7		Royal Saudi AF	F-15D-35-MC	83-0063 – 83-0064	2		Foreign Military Sales (Israel)
F-15B-11-MC	74-139 – 74-140	2			F-15C-30-MC	80-0075 – 80-0085	11		Royal Saudi AF					
F-15B-12-MC	74-141 – 74-142	2			F-15C-31-MC	80-0086 – 80-0099	14		Royal Saudi AF	F-15C-37-MC	84-0001 – 84-0015	15		
F-15A-13-MC	75-0018 – 75-0048	31			F-15C-32-MC	80-0100 – 80-0106	7		Royal Saudi AF	F-15C-38-MC	84-0016 – 84-0031	16		
F-15A-14-MC	75-0049 – 75-0079	31			F-15C-27-MC	80-0107 – 80-0110	4		Royal Saudi AF	F-15D-37-MC	84-0042 – 84-0044	3		
F-15B-13-MC	75-0080 – 75-0084	5			F-15D-28-MC	80-0111 – 80-0112	2		Royal Saudi AF	F-15D-38-MC	84-0045 – 84-0046	2		
F-15B-14-MC	75-0085 – 75-0089	5			F-15D-29-MC	80-0113 – 80-0114	2		Royal Saudi AF	F-15C-39-MC	85-0093 – 85-0107	15		
F-15A-15-MC	76-0008 – 76-0046	39			F-15D-30-MC	80-0115 – 80-0117	3		Royal Saudi AF	F-15C-40-MC	85-0108 – 85-0128	21		
F-15A-16-MC	76-0047 – 76-0083	37			F-15D-31-MC	80-0118 – 80-0119	2		Royal Saudi AF	F-15D-39-MC	85-0129 – 85-0131	3		
F-15A-17-MC	76-0084 – 76-0113	30			F-15D-32-MC	80-0120 – 80-0121	2		Royal Saudi AF	F-15D-40-MC	85-0132 – 85-0134	3		
F-15A-18-MC	76-0114 – 76-0120	7			F-15C-27-MC	80-0122 – 80-0124	3		Foreign Military Sales (Israel)	F-15C-41-MC	86-0143 – 86-0162	20		
F-15B-15-MC	76-0124 – 76-0129	6								F-15C-42-MC	86-0163 – 86-0180	18		
F-15B-16-MC	76-0130 – 76-0135	6			F-15C-28-MC	80-0125 – 80-0127	3		Foreign Military Sales (Israel)	F-15D-41-MC	86-0181 – 86-0182	2		
F-15B-17-MC	76-0136 – 76-0140	5								F-15E-41-MC	86-0183 – 86-0184	2		
F-15B-18-MC	76-0141 – 76-0142	2			F-15C-29-MC	80-0128 – 80-0130	3		Foreign Military Sales (Israel)	F-15E-42-MC	86-0185 – 86-0190	6		
F-15A-17-MC	76-1505 – 76-1514	10		Foreign Military Sales (Israel)						F-15E-43-MC	87-0169 – 87-0189	21		
F-15A-18-MC	76-1515 – 76-1523	9		Foreign Military Sales (Israel)	F-15D-27-MC	80-0131 – 80-0132	2		Foreign Military Sales (Israel)	F-15E-44-MC	87-0190 – 87-0210	21		
F-15B-16-MC	76-1524 – 76-1525	2		Foreign Military Sales (Israel)	F-15D-28-MC	80-0133 – 80-0136	4		Foreign Military Sales (Israel)	F-15E-45-MC	88-1667 – 88-1687	21		
					F-15C-32-MC	81-0002	1		Royal Saudi AF	F-15E-46-MC	88-1688 – 88-1708	21		
F-15A-18-MC	77-0061 – 77-0084	24			F-15C-32-MC	81-0003	1		ex-RSAF, converted to USAF F-15C 81-0056	F-15E-47-MC	89-0046 – 89-0063	18		
F-15A-19-MC	77-0085 – 77-0119	35								F-15E-48-MC	89-0064 – 89-0081	18		
F-15A-20-MC	77-0120 – 77-0153	34			F-15C-30-MC	81-0020 – 81-0031	12							
F-15B-18-MC	77-0154 – 77-0156	3			F-15C-31-MC	81-0032 – 81-0040	9			F-15DJ-24-MC	22-8803 – 22-8806	4		JASDF (as Knock Down Kits to Mitsubishi)
F-15B-19-MC	77-0157 – 77-0162	6			F-15C-32-MC	81-0041 – 81-0055	15							
F-15B-20-MC	77-0163 – 77-0168	6			F-15C-32-MC	81-0056	1		converted from RSAF F-15C 81-0003	F-15DJ-25-MC	22-8807 – 22-8810	4		JASDF (as Knock Down Kits to Mitsubishi)
F-15C-21-MC	78-0468 – 78-0495	28												
F-15C-22-MC	78-0496 – 78-0522	27												

TOTAL ST. LOUIS F-15 PRODUCTION: 1,154

A line-up of Royal Saudi Air Force F-15Cs immediately after delivery by USAF pilots. These aircraft are missing the normal RSAF forward fuselage markings.

F-15A, 73-100, painted by McDonnell Douglas to represent a Royal Saudi Air Force "Eagle". The RSAF eventually received 55 F-15Cs and 17 F-15Ds.

S/MTD AIRCRAFT MODIFICATIONS

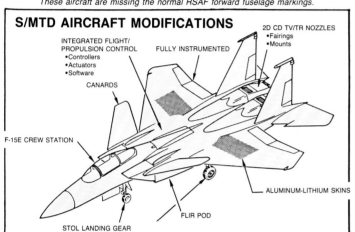

- 2D CD TV/TR NOZZLES
  - Fairings
  - Mounts
- INTEGRATED FLIGHT/PROPULSION CONTROL
  - Controllers
  - Actuators
  - Software
- FULLY INSTRUMENTED
- CANARDS
- F-15E CREW STATION
- ALUMINUM-LITHIUM SKINS
- FLIR POD
- STOL LANDING GEAR

S/MTD NOZZLE OPERATING MODES

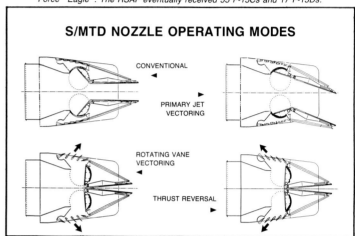

- CONVENTIONAL
- PRIMARY JET VECTORING
- ROTATING VANE VECTORING
- THRUST REVERSAL

PROTOTYPE DATA

Serial No.	McAir No.	First Flight	Function
71-280	F1	7/27/72	Envelope exploration, handling qualities, external stores carriage tests
71-281	F2	9/26/72	F100 engine tests, to NASA
71-282	F3	11/4/72	Avionics development, first AN/APG-63 equipped aircraft, calibrated airspeed tests
71-283	F4	1/13/73	Structural test aircraft
71-284	F5	3/7/73	Internal cannon testing, armament testing, stores jettison tests, first M61 equipped aircraft
71-285	F6	5/23/73	Avionics testing, flight control evaluation, missile firing evaluation, nicknamed "Killer"
71-286	F7	6/14/73	Armament, fuel, and stores testing
71-290	T1	7/7/73	Two-seat evaluation, advanced concepts demonstrator
71-287	F8	8/25/73	Spin tests, high AOA evaluation, to NASA
71-291	T2	10/18/73	Bailed to McAir as demonstrator, *Strike Eagle* prototype
71-288	F9	10/20/73	Integrated airframe/engine evaluations
71-289	F10	1/16/74	Radar and avionics testbed
72-113	F11		Operational tests
72-114	F12		Operational tests (first TEWS equipped aircraft)
72-115	F13		Operational tests
72-116	F14		Climatic (environmental) tests, nicknamed "Homer", to Israel
72-117	F15		Not used in AFDT&E, to Israel
72-118	F16		Operational tests/demonstrations, to Israel
72-119	F17		Project *Streak Eagle*
72-120	F18		Not used in AFDT&E, to Israel

KNOWN F-15 KILLS

Country	Type	Total	Weapon Used
Israel	MiG-21	15.5	6 with *Sparrow*; 4.5 with *Sidewinder/Shafrir*; 2 with M61 20mm; 5 unknown
Israel	MiG-23	3	Unknown
Israel	MiG-25	3	All *Sparrow*
Israel	Other	35	Unknown
KSA	F-4	2	Both with *Sparrow*

USAF F-15 UNITS

Wing	Squadron	Primary Color	Location	Tail Code	F-15 Version	Dates From	To	Comments
1st TFW	27th TFS	yellow	Langley AFB, VA	FF	A/B/C/D	Jan 76	Pres.	12th AF TAC
	71st TFS	red	Langley AFB, VA	FF	A/B/C/D	May 76	Pres.	
	94th TFS	blue	Langley AFB, VA	FF	A/B/C/D	Aug 76	Pres.	
4th TFW	336th TFS	yellow	Seymour-Johnson AFB, NC	SJ	E	Dec 88	Pres.	9th AF TAC
	334th TFS	red	Seymour-Johnson AFB, NC	SJ	E	Oct 89	Pres.	
18th TFW	12th TFS	yellow	Kadena AB, Okinawa	ZZ	C/D	Jan 80	Pres.	5th AF PACAF
	44th TFS	blue	Kadena AB, Okinawa	ZZ	C/D	Oct 79	Pres.	
	67th TFS	red	Kadena AB, Okinawa	ZZ	C/D	Jul 79	Pres.	
21st TFW	43rd TFS	blue	Elmendorf AFB, AK	AK	A/B/C/D	Mar 82	Pres.	Alaskan Air Command
	54th TFS	yellow	Elmendorf AFB, AK	AK	A/B/C/D	Jun 82	Pres.	
33rd TFW	58th TFS	blue	Eglin AFB, FL	EG	A/B/C/D	Jan 79	Pres.	9th AF TAC
	59th TFS	yellow	Eglin AFB, FL	EG	A/B/C/D	Apr 79	Pres.	
	60th TFS	red	Eglin AFB, FL	EG	A/B/C/D	Jun 81	Pres.	
36th TFW	22nd TFS	red	Bitburg AB, Germany	BT	A/B/C/D	Aug 77	Pres.	17th AF USAFE
	53rd TFS	yellow	Bitburg AB, Germany	BT	A/B/C/D	May 77	Pres.	
	525th TFS	blue	Bitburg AB, Germany	BT	A/B/C/D	Dec 76	Pres.	
49th TFW	7th TFS	blue	Holloman AFB, NM	HO	A/B	Oct. 77	Pres.	12th AF TAC
	8th TFS	yellow	Holloman AFB, NM	HO	A/B	Jan 78	Pres.	
	9th TFS	red	Holloman AFB, NM	HO	A/B	Apr 78	Pres.	
57th FWW	422nd TES	black & yellow	Nellis AFB, NV	WA	A/B/C/D	Jun 77	Pres.	USAF TFWC TAC
	USAF FWS	black & yellow	Nellis AFB, NV	WA	A/B/C/D	Nov 76	Pres.	(Ex 433rd FWS)
405th TTW	426th TFTS	red	Luke AFB, AZ	LA	A/B/D	Jan 81	Pres.	12th AF TAC
	461st TFTS	yellow	Luke AFB, AZ	LA	E	Jul 77	Pres.	(originally part of 58th TTW)
	550th TFTS	black	Luke AFB, AZ	LA	A/B/D/E	Sep 77	Pres.	
	555th TFTS	green	Luke AFB, AZ	LA	A/B/D	Nov 74	Pres.	
	4461st TFTS	yellow	Luke AFB, AZ	LA	A/B	Jun 76	Jul 77	
---	32nd TFS	orange	Soesterberg AB, Netherlands	CR	A/B/C/D	Nov 78	Pres.	17th AF USAFE
---	5th FIS	black & yellow	Minot AFB, ND	---	A/B	Dec 84	Apr 88	ADTAC, 1st AF
---	48th FIS	blue	Langley AFB, VA	LY	A/B	Aug 81	Pres.	ADTAC, 1st AF
---	57th FIS	black & white	Keflavik NS, Iceland	IS	A/B/C/D	Jun 84	Pres.	ADTAC, 1st AF
---	318th FIS	blue	McChord AFB, WA	TC	A/B	Jun 83	Oct 89	ADTAC, 1st AF
325th TTW	1st TFTS	red	Tyndall AFB, FL	TY	A/B	Jan 84	Pres.	ADWC
	2nd TFTS	yellow	Tyndall AFB, FL	TY	A/B	May 84	Pres.	
	95th TFTS	blue	Tyndall AFB, FL	TY	A/B	Dec 87	Pres.	
102nd FIW	101st FIS	black	Otis ANGB, MA	---	A/B	Apr 88	Pres.	Massachussets ANG
116th TFW	128th TFS	yellow	Dobbins AFB, Georgia	---	A/B	Jun 86	Pres.	Georgia ANG
142nd FIG	123rd FIS	---	Portland IAP, OR	---	A/B	Aug 89	Pres.	Oregon ANG
154th CompG	199th TFS	---	Hickam AFB, HI	---	A/B	Jun 87	Pres.	Hawaii ANG
159th TFG	122nd TFS	---	NAS New Orleans, LA	---	A/B	Jun 85	Pres.	Louisiana ANG
3246th TW	3247th TS	red & white	Eglin AFB, FL	AD	various	Nov 73	Pres.	Munitions Division
6510th TW	6512th TS	blue & white	Edwards AFB, CA	ED	various	Jul 72	Pres.	F-15 JTF/CTF (AFFTC)
---	448thTS	black & white	Eglin AFB, FL	OT	various	Jun 75	Pres.	TAWC
WRALC	---	red; white & blue	Robins AFB, GA	RG	A	May 78	Pres.	Formerly "WR" tailcode

IN DETAIL:

Jav Miller/Aerofax, Inc.

F-15A cockpit is largely conventional, using only 2 CRTs, one for the TEWS ECM display (right) and one for the Vertical Situation Display (VSD). Originally planned vertical-tape instrumentation was deleted as a cost savings. Radio and IFF controls are located directly below Heads-Up-Display (HUD). Compare size of HUD with later F-15E HUD.

Left side console of F-15A shows throttles, Mode 4 IFF/SIF and Control Augmentation System controls. Cockpit interior is painted overall light gray with flat black panels.

Right side console of F-15A is neatly organized and contains mainly minor controls such as lighting and oxygen. Keypad used to enter navigation data is noteworthy.

A McDonnell Douglas Escapac IC-7 ejection seat is used in all F-15s prior to Block 17. Area behind seat is used for AN/ALQ-135 electronics in single-seat aircraft.

Instrument panel of the F-15B is identical to that of the single-seater. Lack of TEWS scope was common in the F-15A/B due to delays in integrating the ECM equipment.

Front left console of F-15B is also identical to F-15A. Note miscellaneous items such as anti-collision and taxi-lights and air-refueling slipway door controls.

Front right console of F-15B. The F-15B makes an excellent transition trainer since all controls and handling qualities are identical to the single-seat variant.

Rear instrument panel of F-15B contains minimum flight and engine instrumentation. This is sufficient for the instructor pilots for which the back seat was intended.

Left rear console of F-15B contains throttles, integrated communications and ILS/TACAN controls. Circuit breakers and seat height switch are noteworthy.

Right rear console of F-15B contains oxygen and interior lighting controls only. Ejection mode switch forward of console is noteworthy.

F-15A COCKPIT
TYPICAL

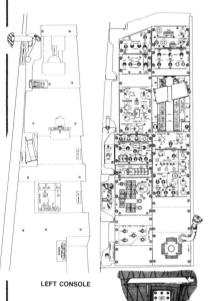

LEFT CONSOLE

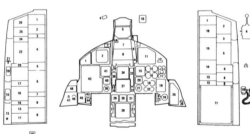

MAIN PANEL

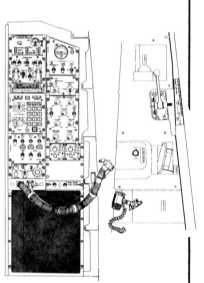

RIGHT CONSOLE

LEFT CONSOLE AREA

1. ILS/TACAN CONTROL PANEL
2. CONTROL AUGMENTATION SYSTEM CONTROL PANEL
3. BLANK
4. THROTTLE QUADRANT
5. EXTERIOR LIGHTS CONTROL PANEL
6. INTEGRATED COMMUNICATIONS CONTROL PANEL
7. BLANK
8. BLANK
9. ANTI-G PANEL
10. BOARDING STEPS POSITION INDICATOR
11. BLANK
12. ARMAMENT SAFETY OVERRIDE SWITCH
13. GROUND POWER PANEL
14. BLANK
15. EMERGENCY AIR REFUELING HANDLE
16. BIT PANEL
17. INTERROGATOR CONTROL PANEL
18. IFF CONTROL PANEL
19. IFF ANTENNA SELECT SWITCH
20. TEWS PANEL
21. SEAT ADJUST SWITCH
22. RADAR ADJUST SWITCH
23. ^{V}MAX SWITCH
24. BLANK
25. FUEL CONTROL PANEL
26. MISCELLANEOUS CONTROL PANEL
27. CANOPY JETTISON HANDLE

MAIN PANEL AREA

1. FIRE WARNING/EXTINGUISHING PANEL
2. VERTICAL SITUATION DISPLAY (VSD)
3. RADIO CONTROL PANEL
4. AIR REFUELING READY LIGHT
5. HEAD UP DISPLAY COMBINING GLASS
6. MASTER CAUTION LIGHT
7. MAIN COMMUNICATIONS CONTROL PANEL
8. HEAD UP DISPLAY CONTROL PANEL
9. GUN SIGHT CAMERA CONTROL PANEL
10. STANDBY MAGNETIC COMPASS
11. TEWS DISPLAY UNIT
12. CANOPY UNLOCKED WARNING LIGHT
13. HYDRAULIC PRESSURE INDICATORS
14. ENGINE TACHOMETERS
15. ALTIMETER
16. FAN TURBINE INLET TEMPERATURE INDICATORS
17. ENGINE OIL PRESSURE INDICATORS
18. FUEL QUANTITY INDICATOR
19. ENGINE FUEL FLOW INDICATORS
20. VERTICAL VELOCITY INDICATOR
21. EIGHT DAY CLOCK
22. ENGINE EXHAUST NOZZLE POSITION INDICATORS
23. JET FUEL STARTER CONTROL HANDLE
24. CABIN PRESSURE ALTIMETER
25. CAUTION LIGHTS PANEL
26. EMERGENCY VENT CONTROL HANDLE
27. CIRCUIT BREAKER PANELS
28. COCKPIT COOLING AND PRESSURIZATION OUTLET
29. STANDBY AIRSPEED INDICATOR
30. STANDBY ATTITUDE INDICATOR
31. STANDBY ALTIMETER
32. RUDDER PEDAL ADJUST RELEASE KNOB

33. MASTER MODE CONTROLS/MARKER BEACON PANEL
34. ATTITUDE DIRECTOR INDICATOR
35. EMERGENCY JETTISON SWITCH
36. STEERING MODE PANEL
37. HORIZONTAL SITUATION INDICATOR
38. EMERGENCY BRAKE/STEERING CONTROL HANDLE
39. ACCELEROMETER
40. ANGLE OF ATTACK INDICATOR
41. AIRSPEED/MACH INDICATOR
42. ARMAMENT CONTROL PANEL
43. PITCH RATIO INDICATOR
44. PITCH RATIO SELECT SWITCH
45. LANDING GEAR CONTROL HANDLE
46. FLAP POSITION INDICATOR
47. EMERGENCY LANDING GEAR HANDLE
48. ARRESTING HOOK CONTROL SWITCH

RIGHT CONSOLE AREA

1. OXYGEN REGULATOR
2. ECS PANEL
3. TEMPERATURE PANEL
4. CANOPY CONTROL HANDLE
5. INTERIOR LIGHTS CONTROL PANEL
6. TEWS POD CONTROL PANEL
7. OXYGEN HOSE STOWAGE FITTING
8. BLANK
9. ENGINE START FUEL SWITCHES
10. UTILITY LIGHT
11. STOWAGE COMPARTMENT
12. OXYGEN/COMMUNICATION OUTLET PANEL
13. COMPASS CONTROL PANEL
14. TEWS POWER CONTROL PANEL
15. NAVIGATION CONTROL PANEL
16. ENGINE CONTROL PANEL

McDonnell Douglas

Dennis R. Jenkins

F-15Bs prior to Block 17 (and all Israeli) use IC-7 ejection seats front and rear. Lever between headrest section "safes" controls when pulled down as shown.

Early F-15 HUD was a vast improvement over previous units, but is now somewhat dated in that it cannot present raster-scan video imagery.

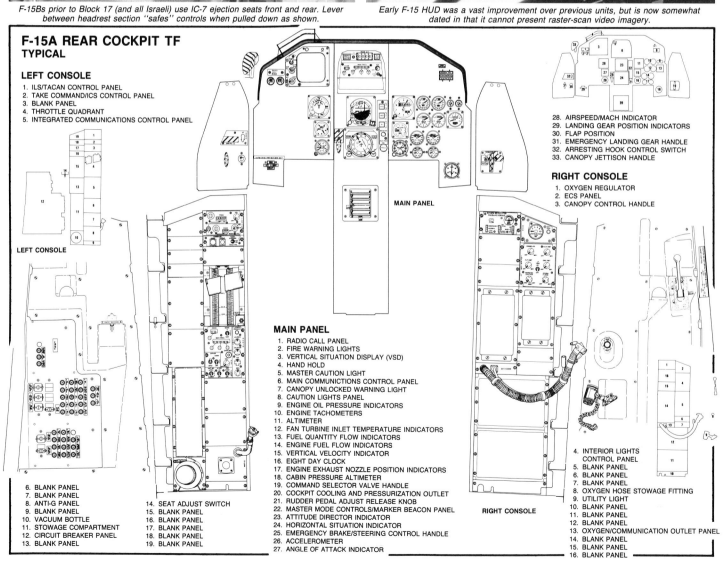

F-15A REAR COCKPIT TF
TYPICAL

LEFT CONSOLE

1. ILS/TACAN CONTROL PANEL
2. TAKE COMMAND/ICS CONTROL PANEL
3. BLANK PANEL
4. THROTTLE QUADRANT
5. INTEGRATED COMMUNICATIONS CONTROL PANEL

LEFT CONSOLE

6. BLANK PANEL
7. BLANK PANEL
8. ANTI-G PANEL
9. BLANK PANEL
10. VACUUM BOTTLE
11. STOWAGE COMPARTMENT
12. CIRCUIT BREAKER PANEL
13. BLANK PANEL

14. SEAT ADJUST SWITCH
15. BLANK PANEL
16. BLANK PANEL
17. BLANK PANEL
18. BLANK PANEL
19. BLANK PANEL

MAIN PANEL

MAIN PANEL

1. RADIO CALL PANEL
2. FIRE WARNING LIGHTS
3. VERTICAL SITUATION DISPLAY (VSD)
4. HAND HOLD
5. MASTER CAUTION LIGHT
6. MAIN COMMUNICTIONS CONTROL PANEL
7. CANOPY UNLOCKED WARNING LIGHT
8. CAUTION LIGHTS PANEL
9. ENGINE OIL PRESSURE INDICATORS
10. ENGINE TACHOMETERS
11. ALTIMETER
12. FAN TURBINE INLET TEMPERATURE INDICATORS
13. FUEL QUANTITY FLOW INDICATORS
14. ENGINE FUEL FLOW INDICATORS
15. VERTICAL VELOCITY INDICATOR
16. EIGHT DAY CLOCK
17. ENGINE EXHAUST NOZZLE POSITION INDICATORS
18. CABIN PRESSURE ALTIMETER
19. COMMAND SELECTOR VALVE HANDLE
20. COCKPIT COOLING AND PRESSURIZATION OUTLET
21. RUDDER PEDAL ADJUST RELEASE KNOB
22. MASTER MODE CONTROLS/MARKER BEACON PANEL
23. ATTITUDE DIRECTOR INDICATOR
24. HORIZONTAL SITUATION INDICATOR
25. EMERGENCY BRAKE/STEERING CONTROL HANDLE
26. ACCELEROMETER
27. ANGLE OF ATTACK INDICATOR

28. AIRSPEED/MACH INDICATOR
29. LANDING GEAR POSITION INDICATORS
30. FLAP POSITION
31. EMERGENCY LANDING GEAR HANDLE
32. ARRESTING HOOK CONTROL SWITCH
33. CANOPY JETTISON HANDLE

RIGHT CONSOLE

1. OXYGEN REGULATOR
2. ECS PANEL
3. CANOPY CONTROL HANDLE

4. INTERIOR LIGHTS
   CONTROL PANEL
5. BLANK PANEL
6. BLANK PANEL
7. BLANK PANEL
8. OXYGEN HOSE STOWAGE FITTING
9. UTILITY LIGHT
10. BLANK PANEL
11. BLANK PANEL
12. BLANK PANEL
13. OXYGEN/COMMUNICATION OUTLET PANEL
14. BLANK PANEL
15. BLANK PANEL
16. BLANK PANEL

RIGHT CONSOLE

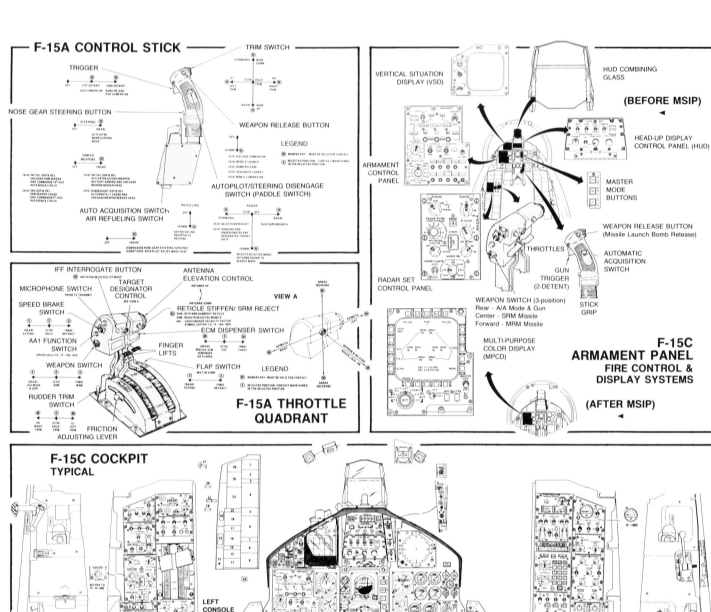

F-15A CONTROL STICK

F-15C ARMAMENT PANEL
FIRE CONTROL & DISPLAY SYSTEMS

F-15A THROTTLE QUADRANT

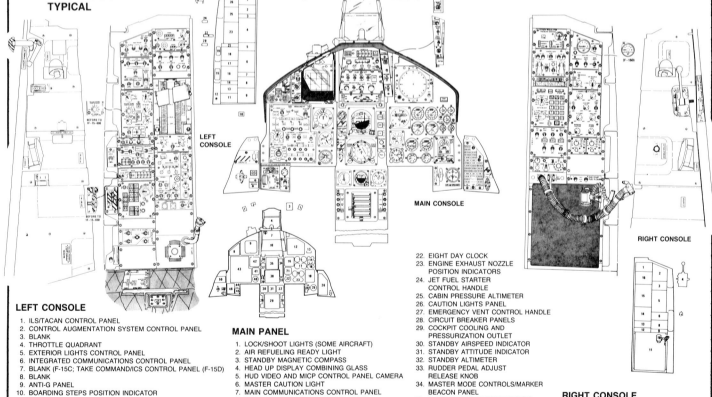

F-15C COCKPIT
TYPICAL

LEFT CONSOLE

1. ILS/TACAN CONTROL PANEL
2. CONTROL AUGMENTATION SYSTEM CONTROL PANEL
3. BLANK
4. THROTTLE QUADRANT
5. EXTERIOR LIGHTS CONTROL PANEL
6. INTEGRATED COMMUNICATIONS CONTROL PANEL
7. BLANK (F-15C; TAKE COMMAND/ICS CONTROL PANEL (F-15D)
8. BLANK
9. ANTI-G PANEL
10. BOARDING STEPS POSITION INDICATOR
11. BLANK
12. ARMAMENT SAFETY OVERRIDE SWITCH
13. GROUND POWER PANEL
14. BLANK
15. EMERGENCY AIR REFUELING SWITCH/HANDLE
16. BIT PANEL
17. INTERROGATOR CONTROL PANEL
18. IFF CONTROL PANEL
19. IFF ANTENNA SELECT SWITCH
20. EWWS ENABLE SWITCH
21. TEWS PANEL
22. SEAT ADJUST SWITCH
23. RADAR CONTROL PANEL
24. MAX SWITCH
25. FUEL CONTROL PANEL
26. MISCELLANEOUS CONTROL PANEL
27. CANOPY JETTISON HANDLE

MAIN PANEL

1. LOCK/SHOOT LIGHTS (SOME AIRCRAFT)
2. AIR REFUELING READY LIGHT
3. STANDBY MAGNETIC COMPASS
4. HEAD UP DISPLAY COMBINING GLASS
5. HUD VIDEO AND MICP CONTROL PANEL CAMERA
6. MASTER CAUTION LIGHT
7. MAIN COMMUNICATIONS CONTROL PANEL
8. FIRE WARNING/EXTINGUISHING PANEL
9. VERTICAL SITUATION DISPLAY (VSD)
10. HEAD UP DISPLAY CONTROL PANEL
11. VIDEO TAPE RECORDER CONTROL PANEL, BLOCK 24 AND UP; GUN SIGHT CAMERA CONTROL PANEL, THRU BLOCK 23
12. TEWS DISPLAY UNIT
13. CANOPY UNLOCKED WARNING LIGHT
14. HYDRAULIC PRESSURE INDICATORS
15. ENGINE TACHOMETERS
16. ALTIMETER
17. FAN TURBINE INLET TEMPERATURE INDICATORS
18. ENGINE OIL PRESSURE INDICATORS
19. FUEL QUANTITY INDICATOR
20. ENGINE FUEL FLOW INDICATORS
21. VERTICAL VELOCITY INDICATOR
22. EIGHT DAY CLOCK
23. ENGINE EXHAUST NOZZLE POSITION INDICATORS
24. JET FUEL STARTER CONTROL HANDLE
25. CABIN PRESSURE ALTIMETER
26. CAUTION LIGHTS PANEL
27. EMERGENCY VENT CONTROL HANDLE
28. CIRCUIT BREAKER PANELS
29. COCKPIT COOLING AND PRESSURIZATION OUTLET
30. STANDBY AIRSPEED INDICATOR
31. STANDBY ATTITUDE INDICATOR
32. STANDBY ALTIMETER
33. RUDDER PEDAL ADJUST RELEASE KNOB
34. MASTER MODE CONTROLS/MARKER BEACON PANEL
35. ATTITUDE DIRECTOR INDICATOR
36. EMERGENCY JETTISON SWITCH
37. STEERING MODE PANEL
38. HORIZONTAL SITUATION INDICATOR
39. EMERGENCY BRAKE/STEERING CONTROL HANDLE
40. ACCELEROMETER
41. ANGLE OF ATTACK INDICATOR
42. AIRSPEED/MACH INDICATOR
43. ARMAMENT CONTROL PANEL
44. PITCH RATIO INDICATOR
45. PITCH RATIO SELECT SWITCH
46. LANDING GEAR CONTROL HANDLE
47. RADIO CALL PANEL
48. FLAP POSITION INDICATOR
49. EMERGENCY LANDING GEAR HANDLE
50. ARRESTING HOOK CONTROL SWITCH

RIGHT CONSOLE

1. OXYGEN
2. ECS PANEL
3. TEMPERATURE PANEL
4. CANOPY CONTROL HANDLE
5. INTERIOR LIGHTS CONTROL PANEL
6. TEWS POD CONTROL PANEL
7. OXYGEN HOSE STOWAGE FITTING
8. BLANK
9. ENGINE START FUEL SWITCHES
10. UTILITY LIGHT
11. STOWAGE COMPARTMENT
12. OXYGEN/COMMUNICATION OUTLET PANEL
13. COMPASS CONTROL PANEL
14. TEWS POWER CONTROL PANEL
15. NAVIGATION CONTROL PANEL
16. ENGINE CONTROL PANEL

Main panel of the prototype F-15A, 71-280. Primary thrust of the instrument complement was test. By the time the "Eagle" had entered full-scale production, much of the panel had undergone considerable change. Only the flight and engine instrument locations remained intact.

Cockpit of F-15C, 80-0017. This same configuration also was found on late-block F-15As. View through single-piece windscreen is superb. HUD is visible mounted above instrument panel.

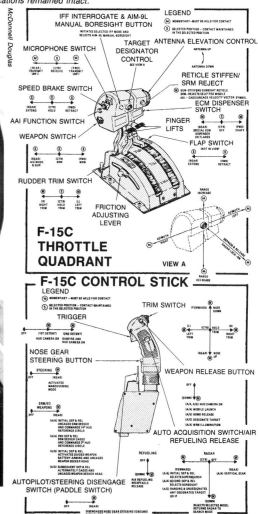

IFF INTERROGATE & AIM-9L MANUAL BORESIGHT BUTTON

LEGEND
(M) MOMENTARY — MUST BE HELD FOR CONTACT
(S) SELECTED POSITION — CONTACT MAINTAINED IN THE SELECTED POSITION

MICROPHONE SWITCH

TARGET DESIGNATOR CONTROL
SEE VIEW A

ANTENNA ELEVATION CONTROL

SPEED BRAKE SWITCH

RETICLE STIFFEN/ SRM REJECT

AAI FUNCTION SWITCH

ECM DISPENSER SWITCH

WEAPON SWITCH

FINGER LIFTS

FLAP SWITCH

RUDDER TRIM SWITCH

FRICTION ADJUSTING LEVER

F-15C THROTTLE QUADRANT

VIEW A

F-15C CONTROL STICK

LEGEND
(M) MOMENTARY — MUST BE HELD FOR CONTACT
(S) SELECTED POSITION — CONTACT MAINTAINED IN THE SELECTED POSITION

TRIGGER

TRIM SWITCH

NOSE GEAR STEERING BUTTON

WEAPON RELEASE BUTTON

AUTO ACQUISITION SWITCH/AIR REFUELING RELEASE

AUTOPILOT/STEERING DISENGAGE SWITCH (PADDLE SWITCH)

F-15D REAR COCKPIT
TYPICAL

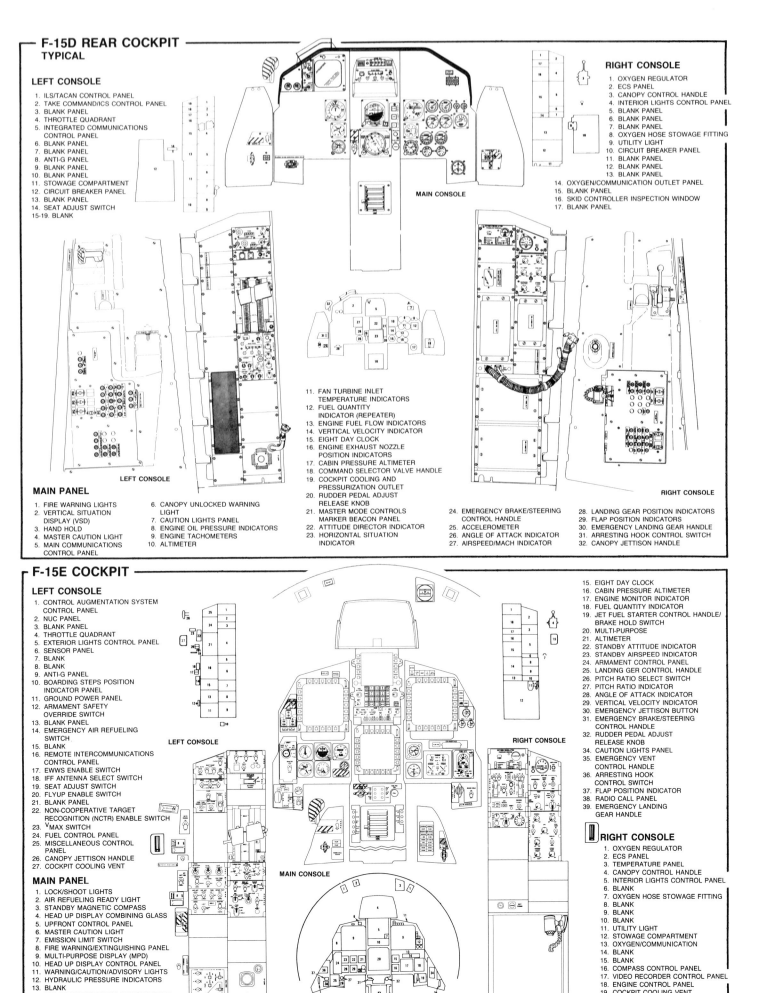

LEFT CONSOLE

1. ILS/TACAN CONTROL PANEL
2. TAKE COMMAND/ICS CONTROL PANEL
3. BLANK PANEL
4. THROTTLE QUADRANT
5. INTEGRATED COMMUNICATIONS CONTROL PANEL
6. BLANK PANEL
7. BLANK PANEL
8. ANTI-G PANEL
9. BLANK PANEL
10. BLANK PANEL
11. STOWAGE COMPARTMENT
12. CIRCUIT BREAKER PANEL
13. BLANK PANEL
14. SEAT ADJUST SWITCH
15-19. BLANK

RIGHT CONSOLE

1. OXYGEN REGULATOR
2. ECS PANEL
3. CANOPY CONTROL HANDLE
4. INTERIOR LIGHTS CONTROL PANEL
5. BLANK PANEL
6. BLANK PANEL
7. BLANK PANEL
8. OXYGEN HOSE STOWAGE FITTING
9. UTILITY LIGHT
10. CIRCUIT BREAKER PANEL
11. BLANK PANEL
12. BLANK PANEL
13. BLANK PANEL
14. OXYGEN/COMMUNICATION OUTLET PANEL
15. BLANK PANEL
16. SKID CONTROLLER INSPECTION WINDOW
17. BLANK PANEL

MAIN PANEL

1. FIRE WARNING LIGHTS
2. VERTICAL SITUATION DISPLAY (VSD)
3. HAND HOLD
4. MASTER CAUTION LIGHT
5. MAIN COMMUNICATIONS CONTROL PANEL
6. CANOPY UNLOCKED WARNING LIGHT
7. CAUTION LIGHTS PANEL
8. ENGINE OIL PRESSURE INDICATORS
9. ENGINE TACHOMETERS
10. ALTIMETER
11. FAN TURBINE INLET TEMPERATURE INDICATORS
12. FUEL QUANTITY INDICATOR (REPEATER)
13. ENGINE FUEL FLOW INDICATORS
14. VERTICAL VELOCITY INDICATOR
15. EIGHT DAY CLOCK
16. ENGINE EXHAUST NOZZLE POSITION INDICATORS
17. CABIN PRESSURE ALTIMETER
18. COMMAND SELECTOR VALVE HANDLE
19. COCKPIT COOLING AND PRESSURIZATION OUTLET
20. RUDDER PEDAL ADJUST RELEASE KNOB
21. MASTER MODE CONTROLS MARKER BEACON PANEL
22. ATTITUDE DIRECTOR INDICATOR
23. HORIZONTAL SITUATION INDICATOR
24. EMERGENCY BRAKE/STEERING CONTROL HANDLE
25. ACCELEROMETER
26. ANGLE OF ATTACK INDICATOR
27. AIRSPEED/MACH INDICATOR
28. LANDING GEAR POSITION INDICATORS
29. FLAP POSITION INDICATORS
30. EMERGENCY LANDING GEAR HANDLE
31. ARRESTING HOOK CONTROL SWITCH
32. CANOPY JETTISON HANDLE

F-15E COCKPIT

LEFT CONSOLE

1. CONTROL AUGMENTATION SYSTEM CONTROL PANEL
2. NUC PANEL
3. BLANK PANEL
4. THROTTLE QUADRANT
5. EXTERIOR LIGHTS CONTROL PANEL
6. SENSOR PANEL
7. BLANK
8. BLANK
9. ANTI-G PANEL
10. BOARDING STEPS POSITION INDICATOR PANEL
11. GROUND POWER PANEL
12. ARMAMENT SAFETY OVERRIDE SWITCH
13. BLANK PANEL
14. EMERGENCY AIR REFUELING SWITCH
15. BLANK
16. REMOTE INTERCOMMUNICATIONS CONTROL PANEL
17. EWWS ENABLE SWITCH
18. IFF ANTENNA SELECT SWITCH
19. SEAT ADJUST SWITCH
20. FLYUP ENABLE SWITCH
21. BLANK PANEL
22. NON-COOPERATIVE TARGET RECOGNITION (NCTR) ENABLE SWITCH
23. VMAX SWITCH
24. FUEL CONTROL PANEL
25. MISCELLANEOUS CONTROL PANEL
26. CANOPY JETTISON HANDLE
27. COCKPIT COOLING VENT

MAIN PANEL

1. LOCK/SHOOT LIGHTS
2. AIR REFUELING READY LIGHT
3. STANDBY MAGNETIC COMPASS
4. HEAD UP DISPLAY COMBINING GLASS
5. UPFRONT CONTROL PANEL
6. MASTER CAUTION LIGHT
7. EMISSION LIMIT SWITCH
8. FIRE WARNING/EXTINGUISHING PANEL
9. MULTI-PURPOSE DISPLAY (MPD)
10. HEAD UP DISPLAY CONTROL PANEL
11. WARNING/CAUTION/ADVISORY LIGHTS
12. HYDRAULIC PRESSURE INDICATORS
13. BLANK
14. DTA TRANSFER MODULE RECEPTACLE

15. EIGHT DAY CLOCK
16. CABIN PRESSURE ALTIMETER
17. ENGINE MONITOR INDICATOR
18. FUEL QUANTITY INDICATOR
19. JET FUEL STARTER CONTROL HANDLE/ BRAKE HOLD SWITCH
20. MULTI-PURPOSE
21. ALTIMETER
22. STANDBY ATTITUDE INDICATOR
23. STANDBY AIRSPEED INDICATOR
24. ARMAMENT CONTROL PANEL
25. LANDING GER CONTROL HANDLE
26. PITCH RATIO SELECT SWITCH
27. PITCH RATIO INDICATOR
28. ANGLE OF ATTACK INDICATOR
29. VERTICAL VELOCITY INDICATOR
30. EMERGENCY JETTISON BUTTON
31. EMERGENCY BRAKE/STEERING CONTROL HANDLE
32. RUDDER PEDAL ADJUST RELEASE KNOB
34. CAUTION LIGHTS PANEL
35. EMERGENCY VENT CONTROL HANDLE
36. ARRESTING HOOK CONTROL SWITCH
37. FLAP POSITION INDICATOR
38. RADIO CALL PANEL
39. EMERGENCY LANDING GEAR HANDLE

RIGHT CONSOLE

1. OXYGEN REGULATOR
2. ECS PANEL
3. TEMPERATURE PANEL
4. CANOPY CONTROL HANDLE
5. INTERIOR LIGHTS CONTROL PANEL
6. BLANK
7. OXYGEN HOSE STOWAGE FITTING
8. BLANK
9. BLANK
10. BLANK
11. UTILITY LIGHT
12. STOWAGE COMPARTMENT
13. OXYGEN/COMMUNICATION
14. BLANK
15. BLANK
16. COMPASS CONTROL PANEL
17. VIDEO RECORDER CONTROL PANEL
18. ENGINE CONTROL PANEL
19. COCKPIT COOLING VENT

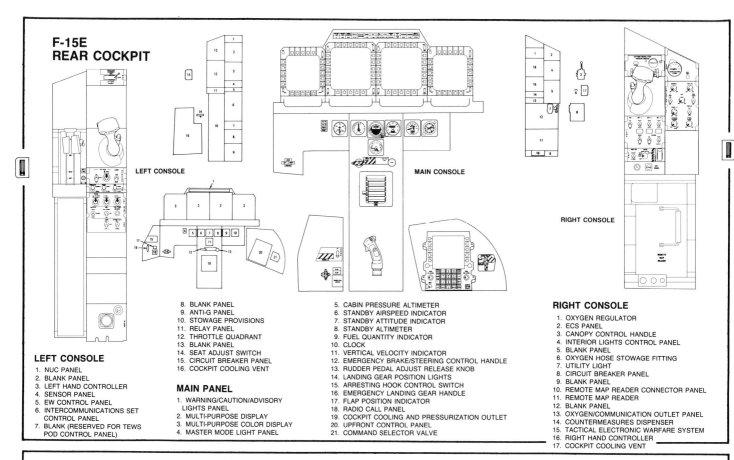

F-15E REAR COCKPIT

LEFT CONSOLE
1. NUC PANEL
2. BLANK PANEL
3. LEFT HAND CONTROLLER
4. SENSOR PANEL
5. EW CONTROL PANEL
6. INTERCOMMUNICATIONS SET CONTROL PANEL
7. BLANK (RESERVED FOR TEWS POD CONTROL PANEL)
8. BLANK PANEL
9. ANTI-G PANEL
10. STOWAGE PROVISIONS
11. RELAY PANEL
12. THROTTLE QUADRANT
13. BLANK PANEL
14. SEAT ADJUST SWITCH
15. CIRCUIT BREAKER PANEL
16. COCKPIT COOLING VENT

MAIN PANEL
1. WARNING/CAUTION/ADVISORY LIGHTS PANEL
2. MULTI-PURPOSE DISPLAY
3. MULTI-PURPOSE COLOR DISPLAY
4. MASTER MODE LIGHT PANEL

MAIN CONSOLE
5. CABIN PRESSURE ALTIMETER
6. STANDBY AIRSPEED INDICATOR
7. STANDBY ATTITUDE INDICATOR
8. STANDBY ALTIMETER
9. FUEL QUANTITY INDICATOR
10. CLOCK
11. VERTICAL VELOCITY INDICATOR
12. EMERGENCY BRAKE/STEERING CONTROL HANDLE
13. RUDDER PEDAL ADJUST RELEASE KNOB
14. LANDING GEAR POSITION LIGHTS
15. ARRESTING HOOK CONTROL SWITCH
16. EMERGENCY LANDING GEAR HANDLE
17. FLAP POSITION INDICATOR
18. RADIO CALL PANEL
19. COCKPIT COOLING AND PRESSURIZATION OUTLET
20. UPFRONT CONTROL PANEL
21. COMMAND SELECTOR VALVE

RIGHT CONSOLE
1. OXYGEN REGULATOR
2. ECS PANEL
3. CANOPY CONTROL HANDLE
4. INTERIOR LIGHTS CONTROL PANEL
5. BLANK PANEL
6. OXYGEN HOSE STOWAGE FITTING
7. UTILITY LIGHT
8. CIRCUIT BREAKER PANEL
9. BLANK PANEL
10. REMOTE MAP READER CONNECTOR PANEL
11. REMOTE MAP READER
12. BLANK PANEL
13. OXYGEN/COMMUNICATION OUTLET PANEL
14. COUNTERMEASURES DISPENSER
15. TACTICAL ELECTRONIC WARFARE SYSTEM
16. RIGHT HAND CONTROLLER
17. COCKPIT COOLING VENT

THROTTLE QUADRANT FRONT

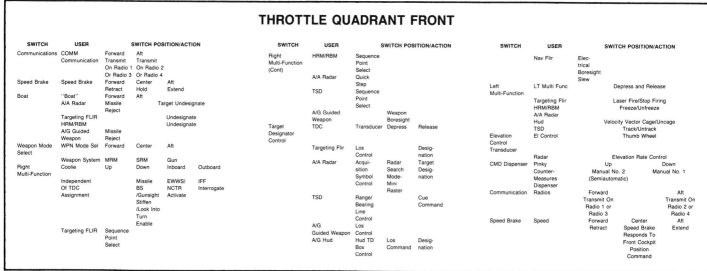

SWITCH	USER	SWITCH POSITION/ACTION		
Communications	COMM Communication	Forward Transmit On Radio 1 Or Radio 3	Aft Transmit On Radio 2 Or Radio 4	
Speed Brake	Speed Brake	Forward Retract	Center Hold	Aft Extend
Boat	"Boat"	Forward	Aft	
	A/A Radar Missile Reject		Target Undesignate	
	Targeting FLIR HRM/RBM		Undesignate	
	A/G Guided Weapon	Missile Reject	Undesignate	
Weapon Mode Select	WPN Mode Sel	Forward	Center	Aft
	Weapon System	MRM	SRM	Gun
Right Multi-Function	Coolie	Up	Down	Inboard Outboard
	Independent Of TDC Assignment	Missile BS /Gunsight Stiffen /Look Into Turn Enable	EWWS/ NCTR Activate	IFF Interrogate
	Targeting FLIR	Sequence Point Select		

SWITCH	USER	SWITCH POSITION/ACTION		
Right Multi-Function (Cont)	HRM/RBM	Sequence Point Select		
	A/A Radar	Quick Step		
	TSD	Sequence Point Select		
	A/G Guided Weapon	Weapon Boresight		
Target Designator Control	TDC	Transducer	Depress	Release
	Targeting Flir	Los Control	Desig- nation	
	A/A Radar	Acqui- sition Symbol Control	Radar Search Mode- Mini Raster	Target Desig- nation
	TSD	Range/ Bearing Line Control		Cue Command
	A/G Guided Weapon	Los Control		
	A/G Hud	Hud TD Box Control	Los Command	Desig- nation

SWITCH	USER	SWITCH POSITION/ACTION		
	Nav Flir	Elec- trical Boresight Slew		
Left Multi-Function	LT Multi Func		Depress and Release	
	Targeting Flir HRM/RBM	Laser Fire/Stop Firing Freeze/Unfreeze		
	A/A Radar Hud	Velocity Vector Cage/Uncage		
	TSD	Track/Untrack Thumb Wheel		
Elevation Control Transducer	El Control			
	Radar	Elevation Rate Control		
CMD Dispenser	Pinky	Up	Down	
	Counter- Measures Dispenser	Manual No. 2 (Semiautomatic)	Manual No. 1	
Communication	Radios	Forward Transmit On Radio 1 or Radio 3		Aft Transmit On Radio 2 or Radio 4
Speed Brake	Speed	Forward Retract	Center Speed Brake Responds To Front Cockpit Position Command	Aft Extend

---

F-15E SENSOR POSITIONING CONTROL

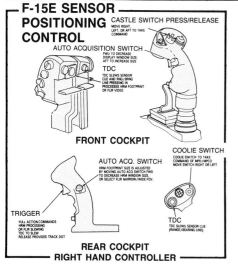

CASTLE SWITCH PRESS/RELEASE
MOVE RIGHT, LEFT, OR AFT TO TAKE COMMAND

AUTO ACQUISITION SWITCH
FWD TO DECREASE DISPLAY WINDOW SIZE, AFT TO INCREASE SIZE

TDC
TDC SLEWS SENSOR CUE AND RNG /BRNG LINE PRESSING IN PROCESSES HRM FOOTPRINT OR FLIR VIDEO

FRONT COCKPIT

AUTO ACQ. SWITCH
HRM FOOTPRINT SIZE IS ADJUSTED BY MOVING AUTO ACQ SWITCH FWD TO DECREASE HRM WINDOW SIZE, OR SELECT FLIR NARROW /WIDE FOV.

COOLIE SWITCH
COOLIE SWITCH TO TAKE COMMAND OF MPD /MPCD MOVE SWITCH RIGHT OR LEFT

TDC
TDC SLEWS SENSOR CUE (RANGE /BEARING LINE)

TRIGGER
FULL ACTION COMMANDS HRM PROCESSING OR FLIR SLEWING TDC TO SLEW RELEASE PROVIDES TRACK DOT

REAR COCKPIT
RIGHT HAND CONTROLLER

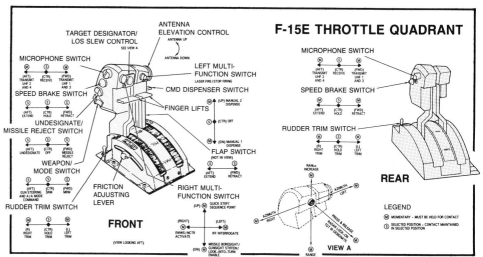

ANTENNA ELEVATION CONTROL
ANTENNA UP
ANTENNA DOWN

TARGET DESIGNATOR/ LOS SLEW CONTROL
SEE VIEW A

MICROPHONE SWITCH
(AFT) TRANSMIT UHF 2 AND 4
(CTR) RECEIVE
(FWD) TRANSMIT UHF 1 AND 3

LEFT MULTI- FUNCTION SWITCH
LASER FIRE /STOP FIRING

CMD DISPENSER SWITCH

FINGER LIFTS

(UP) MANUAL 2 DISPENSE
(S) (CTR) OFF
(M) (DN) MANUAL 1 DISPENSE

SPEED BRAKE SWITCH
(AFT) EXTEND
(CTR) HOLD
(FWD) RETRACT

UNDESIGNATE/ MISSILE REJECT SWITCH
(AFT) UNDESIGNATE
(CTR) OFF
(FWD) MISSILE REJECT

FLAP SWITCH
(NOT IN VIEW)

WEAPON/ MODE SWITCH
(AFT) GUN STEERING AND A/A MODE COMMAND
(CTR) OFF
(FWD) MRM

RUDDER TRIM SWITCH
(R) RIGHT TRIM
(CTR) HOLD TRIM
(L) LEFT TRIM

FRICTION ADJUSTING LEVER

RIGHT MULTI- FUNCTION SWITCH
(UP) QUICK STEP/ SEQUENCE POINT
(RIGHT)
(LEFT)
(M) IFF INTERROGATE
(M) EWWS /NCTR ACTIVATE
(DN) MISSILE BORESIGHT/ GUNSIGHT STIFFEN/ LOOK-INTO-TURN ENABLE

(AFT) RETRACT
(FWD) EXTEND

FRONT

(VIEW LOOKING AFT)

F-15E THROTTLE QUADRANT

MICROPHONE SWITCH
(M) (S) (M)
(AFT) TRANSMIT UHF 2 AND 4
(CTR) RECEIVE
(FWD) TRANSMIT UHF 1 AND 3

SPEED BRAKE SWITCH
(M) (S) (M)
(AFT) EXTEND
(CTR) HOLD
(FWD) RETRACT

RUDDER TRIM SWITCH
(M) (S) (M)
(R) RIGHT TRIM
(CTR) HOLD TRIM
(L) LEFT TRIM

REAR

RANGE INCREASE
AZIMUTH RIGHT
AZIMUTH LEFT
PRESS & RELEASE
RADAR LOCK ON
TGT IR DESIGNATE
RANGE DECREASE

VIEW A

LEGEND
(M) MOMENTARY – MUST BE HELD FOR CONTACT
(S) SELECTED POSITION – CONTACT MAINTAINED IN SELECTED POSITION

The first TF-15A (71-290) was used in a series of tests at Edwards AFB to evaluate rear cockpit conditions with the canopy missing. Early tests used an instrumented dummy in the aft seat although several live pilots later participated in the tests. No actual seat ejections were attempted. Early style pods on vertical stabilizers are noteworthy.

ACES II ejection seat used by USAF F-15s after Block 17. Initiation handles are located on each side of seat.

McDonnell Douglas ACES II seat during ground-based rocket sled test. Two rocket plumes, one directed straight downward and one pushing to the seat forward and up are noteworty. Parachute pack is beginning to deploy.

F-15A
IC-7 EJECTION SEAT

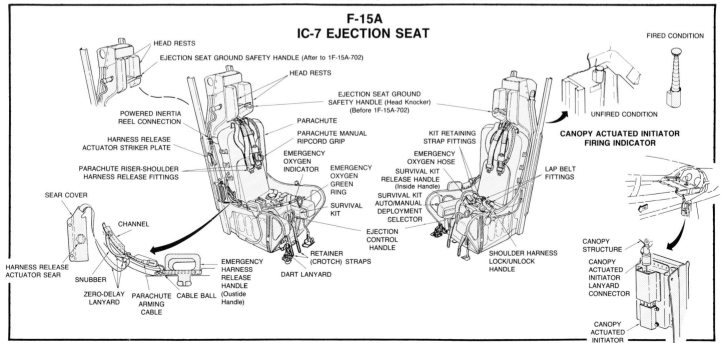

HEAD RESTS

EJECTION SEAT GROUND SAFETY HANDLE (After to 1F-15A-702)

HEAD RESTS

POWERED INERTIA REEL CONNECTION

HARNESS RELEASE ACTUATOR STRIKER PLATE

PARACHUTE RISER-SHOULDER HARNESS RELEASE FITTINGS

SEAR COVER

CHANNEL

HARNESS RELEASE ACTUATOR SEAR

SNUBBER

ZERO-DELAY LANYARD

PARACHUTE ARMING CABLE

CABLE BALL

EMERGENCY HARNESS RELEASE HANDLE (Oustide Handle)

DART LANYARD

RETAINER (CROTCH) STRAPS

EJECTION CONTROL HANDLE

PARACHUTE

PARACHUTE MANUAL RIPCORD GRIP

EMERGENCY OXYGEN INDICATOR

EMERGENCY OXYGEN GREEN RING

SURVIVAL KIT

EJECTION SEAT GROUND SAFETY HANDLE (Head Knocker) (Before 1F-15A-702)

KIT RETAINING STRAP FITTINGS

EMERGENCY OXYGEN HOSE

SURVIVAL KIT RELEASE HANDLE (Inside Handle)

SURVIVAL KIT AUTO/MANUAL DEPLOYMENT SELECTOR

LAP BELT FITTINGS

SHOULDER HARNESS LOCK/UNLOCK HANDLE

FIRED CONDITION

UNFIRED CONDITION

CANOPY ACTUATED INITIATOR FIRING INDICATOR

CANOPY STRUCTURE

CANOPY ACTUATED INITIATOR LANYARD CONNECTOR

CANOPY ACTUATED INITIATOR

F-15C
ACES II EJECTION SEAT

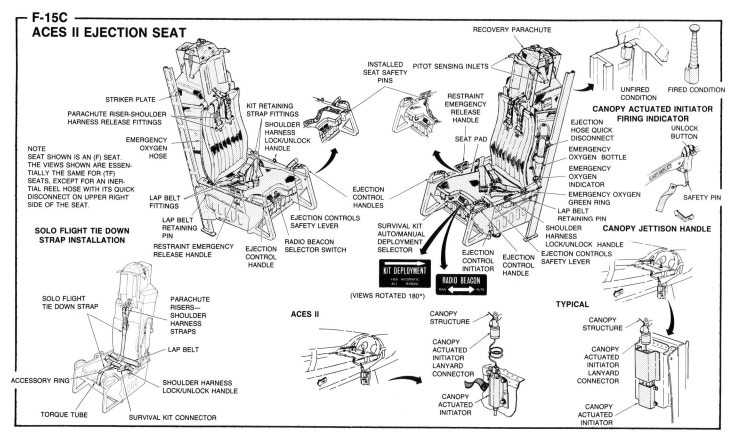

NOTE
SEAT SHOWN IS AN (F) SEAT. THE VIEWS SHOWN ARE ESSENTIALLY THE SAME FOR (TF) SEATS, EXCEPT FOR AN INERTIAL REEL HOSE WITH ITS QUICK DISCONNECT ON UPPER RIGHT SIDE OF THE SEAT.

RECOVERY PARACHUTE

INSTALLED SEAT SAFETY PINS

PITOT SENSING INLETS

STRIKER PLATE

PARACHUTE RISER-SHOULDER HARNESS RELEASE FITTINGS

EMERGENCY OXYGEN HOSE

KIT RETAINING STRAP FITTINGS

SHOULDER HARNESS LOCK/UNLOCK HANDLE

LAP BELT FITTINGS

LAP BELT RETAINING PIN

RESTRAINT EMERGENCY RELEASE HANDLE

EJECTION CONTROL HANDLE

EJECTION CONTROLS SAFETY LEVER

RADIO BEACON SELECTOR SWITCH

EJECTION CONTROL HANDLES

RESTRAINT EMERGENCY RELEASE HANDLE

SEAT PAD

SURVIVAL KIT AUTO/MANUAL DEPLOYMENT SELECTOR

KIT DEPLOYMENT
FWD AUTOMATIC
AFT MANUAL

RADIO BEACON
MAN ◄——► AUTO

(VIEWS ROTATED 180°)

ACES II

EJECTION CONTROL INITIATOR

EJECTION CONTROL HANDLE

UNFIRED CONDITION

FIRED CONDITION

CANOPY ACTUATED INITIATOR FIRING INDICATOR

EJECTION HOSE QUICK DISCONNECT

EMERGENCY OXYGEN BOTTLE

EMERGENCY OXYGEN INDICATOR

EMERGENCY OXYGEN GREEN RING

LAP BELT RETAINING PIN

SHOULDER HARNESS LOCK/UNLOCK HANDLE

EJECTION CONTROLS SAFETY LEVER

UNLOCK BUTTON

SAFETY PIN

CANOPY JETTISON HANDLE

SOLO FLIGHT TIE DOWN STRAP INSTALLATION

SOLO FLIGHT TIE DOWN STRAP

PARACHUTE RISERS— SHOULDER HARNESS STRAPS

LAP BELT

ACCESSORY RING

SHOULDER HARNESS LOCK/UNLOCK HANDLE

TORQUE TUBE

SURVIVAL KIT CONNECTOR

CANOPY STRUCTURE

CANOPY ACTUATED INITIATOR LANYARD CONNECTOR

CANOPY ACTUATED INITIATOR

TYPICAL

CANOPY STRUCTURE

CANOPY ACTUATED INITIATOR LANYARD CONNECTOR

CANOPY ACTUATED INITIATOR

George Cockle

A boarding ladder is built into the left side of the aircraft but is seldom used.

George Cockle

7112

Nose radome is constructed of dielectric materials with a small metal tip. The latter rarely color-matches the rest of the radome. Radome is hinged and opens to starboard side of aircraft.

Large canopy gives the F-15 pilot excellent 360° visibility. Mirrors on inside of canopy rail are noteworthy. One-piece forward windscreen aids visibility.

George Cockle

The two-seater's canopy has slightly different contours to provide additional headroom for the back-seater. Windscreen is identical to the single-seater.

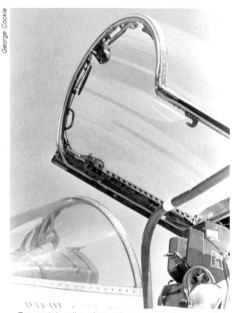

There is no interior windscreen separating the back seat from the front seat. This can lead to the back seat pilot also being incapacitated in the event of a bird strike. Five locking hooks on each side of canopy frame are noteworthy.

Two grab-handles, three mirrors, a standby magnetic compass and caution lights are on the canopy bow.

Underside of the single-seat canopy shows construction details. The support at forward end is not the actuator, and is manually installed after canopy is raised. Mechanism at upper end of support rod is used to lock canopy closed.

The forward canopy section on the single-seater is significantly bulged compared to the aft section.

The two-position trailing edge flaps are mounted inbound of the aileron and a fuel dump is visible just outboard of the aileron. The flaps, aileron and wingtip are liberally marked with ''no-step'' that indicates their unreinforced composite-honeycomb construction. Old-style national insignia and quantity of miscellaneous markings are noteworthy.

The F-15 wing is a model of simplicity, containing only a trailing-edge flap and aileron, with no high-lift devices. Anti-collision light on leading edge near root and old-style national insignia are noteworthy.

Note AN/ALR-56 antenna just inboard of the position light and electroluminescent formation light strip.

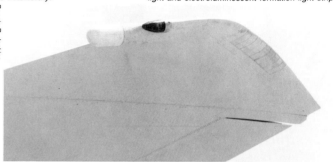

The prototype aircraft were initially delivered with a "square" wingtip (left) that caused a severe buffeting at certain airspeeds. Engineers at Edwards found cutting 3 sq. ft. of the tip off (right) cured the problem. Wood filler was used at first to smooth the wingtips of aircraft modified at Edwards prior to the installation of production-style wingtips.

The second F-15A (71-281) was used by NASA to evaluate aerodynamic effects on Space Shuttle "tiles". The tiles (black area) were mounted in a fiberglass glove that faired them into the F-15's wing. During the flight test program the tiles were subjected to higher pressures and temperatures than those expected during Shuttle ascent.

The first three F-15 prototypes used a horizontal stabilator (without the notch in the leading edge) that caused a mild flutter, leading to the current stabilator design. Stabilators are capable of moving asymmetrically. The only location approved as a walkway on the stabilator is the small area enclosed in the black rectangle at the root.

The F-15 vertical stabilizers have been equipped with several pods. A harmonic balancer is on the right fin-tip and and ECM pod containing aft-looking AN/ALQ-128 antennas is on the left fin-tip. Foreign aircraft generally have harmonic balancers on both sides and early aircraft had different dummy pods on both sides.

This F-15B (73-107) has a late-style ECM pod on the left fin-tip and an early-style dummy pod on the right. Markings are for the Luke AFB Commanding Officer.

A late-style ECM pod is on top of the vertical stabilizer. Immediately below it on the trailing edge is an AN/ALR-56 antenna and below that is a position light.

The first prototype (71-280) shows the original small speed brake in a partially extended position. This speed brake design caused mild buffeting when fully extended.

The first F-15E (86-0183) during construction gives details of the production speed brake design. This design was incorporated on 73-085 and subsequent aircraft.

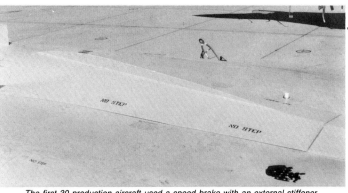

The first 30 production aircraft used a speed brake with an external stiffener. Subsequent aircraft used different construction that deleted the need for the stiffener.

The left glove section contains the air-refueling door (lighter area). A UHF/VHF blade antenna is on the upper fuselage ahead of the speed brake.

All F-15s prior to the F-15E used a two-panel electroluminescent formation light strip on the rear fuselage just below the vertical stabilizer leading edge.

The upper and lower aft fuselage of all F-15s is left unpainted due to the temperatures generated by the engines. Note hot air exhaust immediately below light strip.

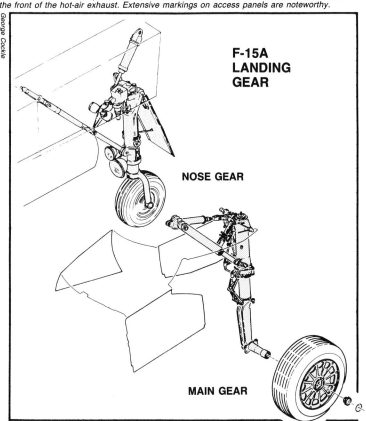

A small strake was added immediately above the front of each aft AIM-7 attach point to assure clean missile separation at launch. Air intakes and a fire access door are located above the rear of AIM-7 attach point. Fairing on underside of fuselage extension is the front of the hot-air exhaust. Extensive markings on access panels are noteworthy.

F-15A LANDING GEAR

NOSE GEAR

MAIN GEAR

Wing glove-fairing is a complex structure. The right side houses the M61A1 20mm "Vulcan" cannon, although the ammunition is stored in the center fuselage.

Front landing gear is fairly simple and retracts forward. The large gear door remains closed except during operation. Taxi (upper) and landing (lower) lights are mounted on gear strut. Aircraft serial number is usually stenciled on inside of auxiliary door. Minor variations between early-model F-15s (right) and F-15E (left) are noteworthy.

Several styles of main wheels have been used over the years. The wheels are functionally identical and are interchangeable (except for F-15E). Various units have painted the wheels in a variety of colors although they are normally either white or black. Tires come from various manufacturers such as Goodyear (left) and B. F. Goodrich (right).

Main landing gear is also simple and retracts forward after the wheel assembly rotates 90°. The two-section main gear doors are normally closed except when the landing gear is extending or retracting, leaving only the small auxiliary door open. Note ground clearance under centerline fuel tank. Center of wheel is occasionally decorated with designs.

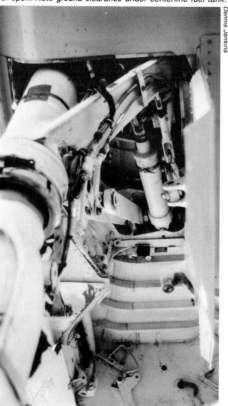

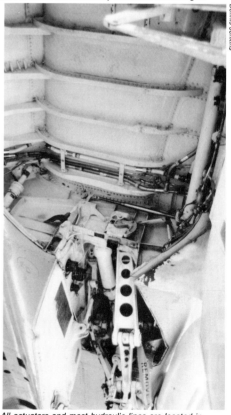

Small auxiliary door is mechanically linked to gear strut and closes as gear retracts.

Forward section of main wheel well is essentially empty. All actuators and most hydraulic lines are located in small aft portion of gear well. Interior of gear wells and doors and all struts are painted gloss white.

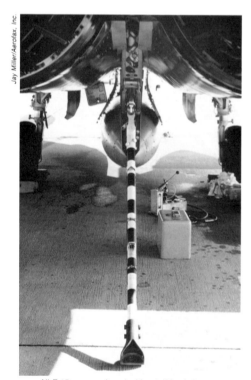

All F-15s are equipped with a tail hook for emergency arrested landings. Early aircraft had doors to cover the hook portion in its retracted position, but these were deleted to simplify maintenance. A fixed "door" covers the majority of the assembly and is usually painted, unlike the surrounding area. The tail hook is black and white striped.

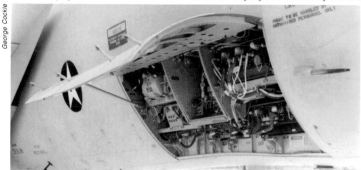

Hinged panels on the forward nose section permit access to radar hardware, various avionics components, and some environmental control items (for rack area cooling). Almost all components consist of line replaceable black boxes and related accessories.

Large upward-hinged access panels are provided for all forward avionics and equipment bays. The bulged cover on the raised forward door covers the pitot-static tube, while the cover immediately aft of the open bay protects the angle-of-attack sensor. There is a duplicate set of sensors on the other side of the fuselage.

The large radome is hinged on the right to provide access to the AN/APG-63 (or AN/APG-70) antenna. (Photo at left shows protective cover on antenna.) All of the radar electronic components are housed in the left forward avionics bay. Note support rods at bottom of radome and forward edge of avionics bay door to keep them open.

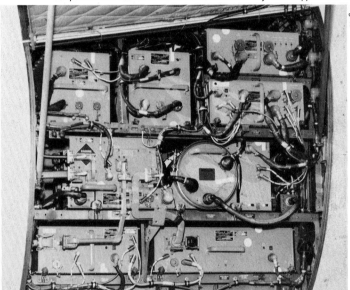

F-15A/Bs and early F-15C/Ds use a Hughes AN/APG-63 radar consisting of seven LRUs plus the antenna. F-15C/Ds processed through MSIP-II use an AN/APG-70 radar.

Late F-15C/Ds and all F-15Es use an upgraded AN/APG-70 radar. This unit deleted the analog signal processor that occupied the upper left position in the avionics bay.

F-15A RADAR SET INSTALLATION

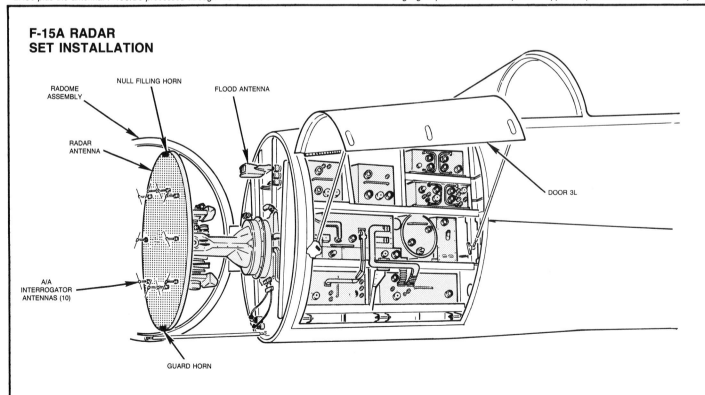

RADOME ASSEMBLY

NULL FILLING HORN

FLOOD ANTENNA

RADAR ANTENNA

DOOR 3L

A/A INTERROGATOR ANTENNAS (10)

GUARD HORN

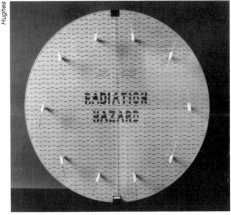

POWER SUPPLY 3173610

ANALOG SIGNAL PROCESSOR 3173039

RADAR DATA PROCESSOR 3173081

RADAR SIGNAL PROCESSOR 3173042

ANTENNA 3173031

TRANSMITTER 3173011

CONTROL 3173541

RECEIVER 3173022

EXCITER 3173001

The original Hughes AN/APG-63 high frequency, pulse-Doppler attack radar as installed in the F-15A/B and early F-15C/Ds. All radar LRUs are located in the left forward avionics bay. The upgraded AN/APG-70 unit utilizes the same antenna and power supply, but replaces or modifies all other components. Radar video is presented on cockpit VSD.

A/A MODES RADAR SEARCH PARAMETERS

A/A MODE	RANGE/VELOCITY SCALES SELECTABLE	ANTENNA SCAN (SEARCH) AZ SCAN	EL BARS	VSD DISPLAY
Long Range[1] Search (LRS) HI/MED PRF	10, 20, 40, 80, or 160 NM	120°, 60° or 20°	1, 2, 4, 6 or 8 Bars	B-Scan, Space-Stabilized. Up to 7 Frame Data Aging
Velocity Search (VS) HI PRF	Search: RNG Scale, 80 to 1800 kts TGT Relative GS[2] Track: 10, 20, 40, 80, or 160 NM	Same as LRS		Same as LRS except during search, TGT Relative GS instead of RNG
Short Range Search (SRS) MED PRF	Search: 10, 20, 40 NM Track: 10, 20, 40, 80 or 160 NM	Same as LRS		Same as LRS
Pulse Search[3] LO PRF	10, 20, 40, 80 or 160 NM	Same as LRS		B-Scan, Space-Stabilized No Data Aging
Beacon[3] LO PRF	10, 20, 40, 80 or 160 NM	Same As LRS		B-Scan, Space Stabilized

[1]MED PRF only in 10 NM range. HI PRF only in 160 NM range.
[2]Velocity coverage is 380 to 2100 KTS in 160 NM range.
[3]Mode not operable in aircraft with 16K radar data processor.

RADIATION HAZARD

Planer array antenna is common between the AN/APG-63 and AN/APG-70.

Prototypes were equipped with a test boom with beta and alpha vanes plus additional pitot-static ports. Later test aircraft, such as the first F-15C, have also used booms.

71-287 used this massive nose boom during an early test program with NASA/Dryden. The majority of test instrumentation is hidden by protective covers.

57

The F-15's intakes are capable of individually pivoting from 11° below the horizontal to 4° above to provide optimal subsonic airflow to the engines.

The intakes are well separated from the fuselage to avoid the boundary-layer air. The large upper surface of the inlet provides a measurable amount of lift to the aircraft.

The inlets pivot about a hinge at the bottom forward lip. Note the unpainted "wedge" that shows the extent of possible movement. Each inlet consists of three variable position ramps, a variable diffuser ramp, and a variable by-pass door. The inlets are stall-free at any flight attitude and all altitudes. Old-style national insignia in both photos is noteworthy.

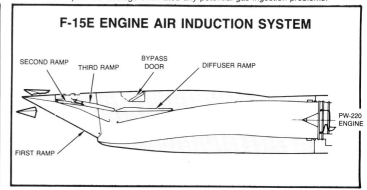

It is normal to see the intake in the full down position while the aircraft is taxiing. When the aircraft rotates, this places the top of the intake parallel to the angle of flight.

The large vent in the lower left is the M61A1 20 mm cannon exhaust port. Placing it on top of the fuselage eliminated any potential gas ingestion problems.

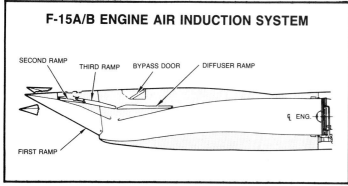

F-15A/B ENGINE AIR INDUCTION SYSTEM

SECOND RAMP THIRD RAMP BYPASS DOOR DIFFUSER RAMP

FIRST RAMP

ENG.

F-15E ENGINE AIR INDUCTION SYSTEM

SECOND RAMP THIRD RAMP BYPASS DOOR DIFFUSER RAMP

FIRST RAMP

PW-220 ENGINE

58

This F100 engine will be raised about 2 ft. to match rails barely visible in the engine bay. Engines are interchangeable left and right since all accessories are on the AMAD.

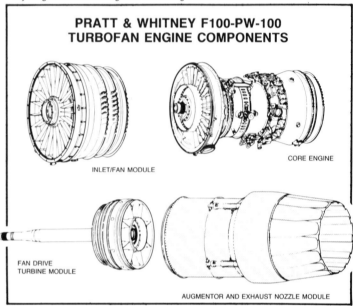

PRATT & WHITNEY F100-PW-100 TURBOFAN ENGINE COMPONENTS

INLET/FAN MODULE

CORE ENGINE

FAN DRIVE TURBINE MODULE

AUGMENTOR AND EXHAUST NOZZLE MODULE

Large access doors ease maintenance on the F100 engines. The engine itself slides rearward on rails located at bottom of the engine bay for removal and installation.

The F100-PW-100 second-generation fighter turbofan engine was developed as a result of continuing problems encountered with the TF30 turbofans installed in the F-111. The titanium "turkey feathers" surrounding the exhaust nozzle were expensive ($1,200) and a maintenance headache, and were often left off operational engines.

The improved F100-PW-220 introduced digital engine controllers to eliminate a persistent stall-stagnation problem on the original F100-PW-100. The engine produces slightly less thrust but offers greater fuel economy, faster throttle response, and increased interval between overhauls. The F100-PW-220 is not equipped with "turkey feathers".

Pratt & Whitney

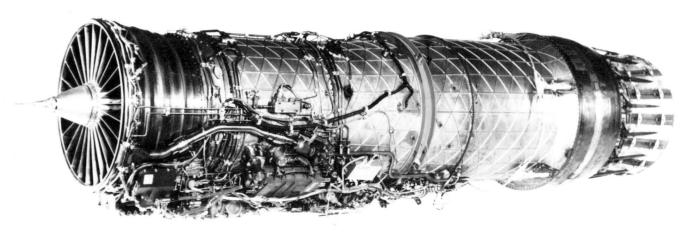

An effort to increase the performance of both the F-15 and F-16 has resulted in the development of the F100-PW-229. This engine produces in excess of 5,000 lbs. more thrust than the F100-PW-220 with no significant fuel consumption or reliability penalties. The first F-15E equipped with F100-PW-229 engines was delivered during late-1989.

McDonnell Douglas

Dennis R. Jenkins

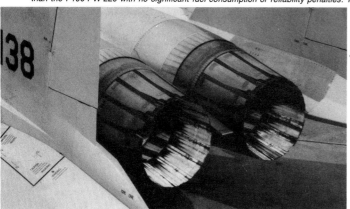

These F100-PW-100 engines show the configuration of the "turkey feathers" when installed. Note the unpainted areas forward of and on the side of the engine nozzles.

The complexity of the F100's convergent-divergent axisymmetric exhaust nozzle is readily apparent when the "turkey feathers" are removed.

George Cockle

Don Logan

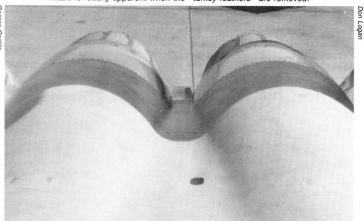

The F-15 engines use a fire extinguishing system and are separated by a titanium keel structure that protects each engine in the event of a catastrophic failure of the other.

The upper fuselage is highly sculptured to accommodate the two F100 engines. The unpainted areas forward of the exhaust nozzles are noteworthy.

George Cockle

The 610 gal. external fuel tank is rated at 9 g's when empty, the same as the basic F-15 airframe. This allows the F-15 to engage in aerial combat without jettisoning the external tanks. The same tank is utilized on all three stores stations. F-4G "Wild Weasel" aircraft also use this tank on their centerline station.

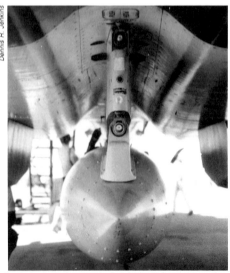

The tank is attached with two lugs on the upper centerline and a single pivot point on the aft of the rear fin. This assures the tank pivots downward when jettisoned and does not strike the underside of the aircraft. Note non-flush rivets on aft end of tank, out the critical airflow. A centerline tank is carried on most flights by operational F-15 units.

The external tank does not interfere with carrying AIM-9 or AIM-120As on the inboard wing pylons. Photo reference markings on pylon of No. 13 prototype are noteworthy.

The conformal fuel tank bolts to the side of each intake trunk, thus freeing up the pylons for weapons. This is a type-1 CFT not equipped for tangential weapon carriage.

The conformal fuel tanks (FAST Packs) are installed using standard AF bomb lift trucks with an adapter. The CFTs actually slide up on rails built into the aircraft's intake trunks and secure with two bolts. Fluid and electrical connections mounted along the top edge of the CFT are made automatically as the CFT slides into place.

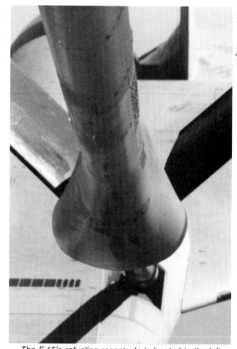

Type-4 CFTs used on F-15Es are equipped for tangential carriage. LANTIRN pods beneath air intakes and the mix of AIM-9s and AIM-120As on the wing pylons are noteworthy.

The F-15's refueling receptacle is located in the left wing glove and is clearly visible from the cockpit.

F-15A FUEL QUANTITY DATA TABLE JP-4

TANK		USABLE FUEL		
		GALLONS	POUNDS AT 6.5 LB/GAL	POUNDS AT 6.3 LB/GAL
TANK 1 [2]		485	3150 ± 100	3050 ± 100
RIGHT ENG FEED TANK		242	1550 ± 100	1520 ± 100
LEFT ENG FEED TANK		186	1200 ± 100	1170 ± 100
INTERNAL WING TANKS	L	423	2750 ± 200	2660 ± 200
	R	423	2750 ± 200	2660 ± 200
TOTAL INTERNAL FUEL		1759	11,400 ± 450	11,060 ± 450
EXTERNAL WING TANKS	L	610	3950 ± 250	3840 ± 250
	R	610	3950 ± 250	3840 ± 250
INTERNAL FUEL PLUS EXTERNAL WING TANKS		2979	19,300 ± 600	18,740 ± 600
EXTERNAL ₵ TANK		610	3950 ± 250	3840 ± 250
INTERNAL FUEL PLUS EXTERNAL ₵ TANK		2369	15,350 ± 500	14,900 ± 500
MAXIMUM FUEL LOAD TOTAL INTERNAL PLUS ALL EXTERNAL TANKS		3589	23,250 ± 650	22,580 ± 650

NOTE

THE FUEL QUANTITIES, IN POUNDS, ARE ROUNDED OFF TO READABLE VALUES OF COUNTER PORTION OF THE FUEL QUANTITY INDICATOR; THEREFORE, THE ACTUAL GALLONS TIMES 6.5 OR 6.3 WILL NOT NECESSARILY AGREE WITH THE POUNDS COLUMN.

FUEL WEIGHTS ARE BASED ON JP-4 AT 6.5 AND 6.3 POUNDS PER GALLON (DIFFERENCES ARE DUE TO MANUFACTURERS' ALLOWABLE TOLERANCES) AND 65 DEGREES FAHRENHEIT.

[1] CALCULATED VALUES

[2] ON AIRPLANES BLOCK 10 AND UP, ADD APPROXIMATELY 200 POUNDS TO THE VALUES FOR TANK 1.

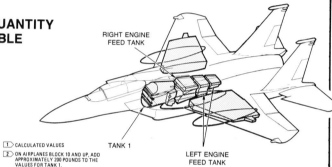

RIGHT ENGINE FEED TANK

TANK 1

LEFT ENGINE FEED TANK

F-15C FUEL QUANTITY DATA TABLE — JP-4 OR JP-8

LEFT ENGINE FEED TANK

RIGHT ENGINE FEED TANK

TANK 1

TANK		USABLE FUEL			
		GALLONS	JP-4 POUNDS AT 6.5 LB/GAL	JP-4 POUNDS AT 6.3 LB/GAL	JP-8 POUNDS AT 6.7 LB/GAL
TANK 1		655	4250 ± 170	4150 ± 170	4400 ± 170
RIGHT ENG FEED (TANK 2)		234	1500 ± 110	1450 ± 110	1550 ± 110
LEFT ENG FEED (TANK 3)		189	1250 ± 105	1150 ± 105	1250 ± 105
INTERNAL WING TANKS	L	496	3200 ± 270	3150 ± 270	3300 ± 270
	R	496	3200 ± 270	3150 ± 270	3300 ± 270
INTERNAL FUEL LESS CONFORMAL TANKS		2070	13,450 ± 480	13,050 ± 480	13,850 ± 480
EXTERNAL WING TANKS	L	610	3950 ± 300	3800 ± 300	4100 ± 300
	R	610	3950 ± 300	3800 ± 300	4100 ± 300
INT FUEL PLUS EXT WING TANKS LESS CONFORMAL TANKS		3290	21,400 ± 850	20,750 ± 850	22,050 ± 850
EXTERNAL ₵ TANK		610	3950 ± 300	3800 ± 300	4100 ± 300
INT FUEL PLUS EXT ₵ TANK LESS CONFORMAL TANKS		2680	17,400 ± 770	16,900 ± 770	17,950 ± 770
INT FUEL PLUS 3 EXT TANKS LESS CONFORMAL TANKS		3900	25,350 ± 940	24,550 ± 940	26,150 ± 940
CONFORMAL TANKS	L	*	*	*	*
	R	*	*	*	*
INTERNAL FUEL PLUS CONFORMAL TANKS		*	*	*	*
INT FUEL PLUS EXT WING TANKS AND CONFORMAL TANKS		*	*	*	*
INT FUEL PLUS EXT ₵ TANK AND CONFORMAL TANKS		*	*	*	*
MAX FUEL LOAD— INT FUEL PLUS 3 EXT TANKS AND CONFORMAL TANKS		*	*	*	*

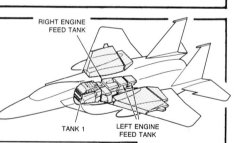

NOTES

THE FUEL QUANTITIES, IN POUNDS, ARE ROUNDED OFF TO READABLE VALUES OF COUNTER PORTION OF THE FUEL QUANTITY INDICATOR; THEREFORE, THE ACTUAL GALLONS TIMES 6.5, 6.3 OR 6.7 WILL NOT NECESSARILY AGREE WITH THE POUNDS COLUMN.

FUEL WEIGHTS ARE BASED ON JP-8 AT 6.7 AND JP-4 AT 6.5 AND 6.3 POUNDS PER GALLON (DIFFERENCES ARE DUE TO MANUFACTURERS' ALLOWABLE TOLERANCES) AND 65 DEGREES FAHRENHEIT.

[1] ESTIMATED VALUES

* TO BE SUPPLIED WHEN AVAILABLE

F-15E FUEL QUANTITY DATA TABLE

RIGHT ENGINE FEED TANK

TANK 1

LEFT ENGINE FEED TANK

NOTES

THE FUEL QUANTITIES, POUNDS, ARE ROUNDED OFF TO READABLE VALUES OF COUNTER PORTION OF THE FUEL QUANTITY INDICATOR;

TANK		USABLE FUEL				
		GALLONS	JP-4 POUNDS AT 6.5 LB/GAL	JP-8 POUNDS AT 6.3 LB/GAL	JP-8 POUNDS AT 6.7 LB/GAL	JP-5 POUNDS AT 6.8 LB/GAL
TANK 1		604	3,900 ± 150	3,800 ± 150	4,050 ± 150	4,100 ± 150
RIGHT ENG FEED (TANK 2)		234	1,500 ± 100	1,450 ± 100	1,550 ± 100	1,590 ± 100
LEFT ENG FEED (TANK 3)		189	1,250 ± 100	1,150 ± 100	1,250 ± 100	1,290 ± 100
INTERNAL WING TANKS	L	496	3,200 ± 250	3,150 ± 250	3,300 ± 250	3,370 ± 250
	R	496	3,200 ± 250	3,150 ± 250	3,300 ± 250	3,370 ± 250
INTERNAL FUEL LESS CONFORMAL TANKS		2,019	13,100 ± 500	12,700 ± 500	13,550 ± 500	13,750 ± 500
EXTERNAL WING TANKS	L	610	3,950 ± 300	3,800 ± 300	4,100 ± 300	4,150 ± 300
	R	610	3,950 ± 300	3,800 ± 300	4,100 ± 300	4,150 ± 300
INT FUEL PLUS EXT WING TANKS LESS CONFORMAL TANKS		3,239	21,050 ± 850	20,400 ± 850	21,700 ± 850	22,000 ± 850
EXTERNAL ₵ TANK		610	3,950 ± 300	3,800 ± 300	4,100 ± 300	4,150 ± 300
INT FUEL PLUS EXT ₵ TANK LESS CONFORMAL TANKS		2,629	17,100 ± 750	16,550 ± 750	17,600 ± 750	17,900 ± 750
INT FUEL PLUS 3 EXT TANKS LESS CONFORMAL TANKS		3,849	25,000 ± 950	24,250 ± 950	25,800 ± 950	26,150 ± 950
CONFORMAL TANKS	L	728	4,750 ± 300	4,600 ± 300	4,900 ± 300	4,950 ± 300
	R	728	4,750 ± 300	4,600 ± 300	4,900 ± 300	4,950 ± 300
INTERNAL FUEL PLUS CONFORMAL TANKS		3,475	22,600 ± 900	21,900 ± 900	23,300 ± 900	23,650 ± 900
INT FUEL PLUS EXT WING TANKS AND CONFORMAL TANKS		4,695	30,500 ± 1050	29,600 ± 1050	31,450 ± 1050	31,950 ± 1050
INT FUEL PLUS EXT ₵ TANK AND CONFORMAL TANKS		4,085	26,550 ± 950	25,750 ± 950	27,350 ± 950	27,800 ± 950
MAX FUEL LOAD—INT FUEL PLUS 3 EXT TANKS AND CONFORMAL TANKS		5,305	34,500 ± 1150	33,400 ± 1150	35,550 ± 1150	36,100 ± 1150

THEREFORE, THE ACTUAL GALLONS TIMES 6.5, 6.3, 6.7 OR 6.8 WILL NOT NECESSARILY AGREE WITH THE POUNDS COLUMN.

FUEL WEIGHTS ARE BASED ON JP-5 AT 6.8, JP-8 AT 6.7 AND JP-4 AT 6.5 AND 6.3 POUNDS PER GALLON (DIFFERENCES ARE DUE TO MANUFACTURERS' ALLOWABLE TOLERANCES) AND 65 DEGREES FAHRENHEIT.

The nozzle for the M61A1 20 mm cannon is located in the right wing glove, slightly aft of the intake. This eliminates possible stall-producing gas ingestion problems.

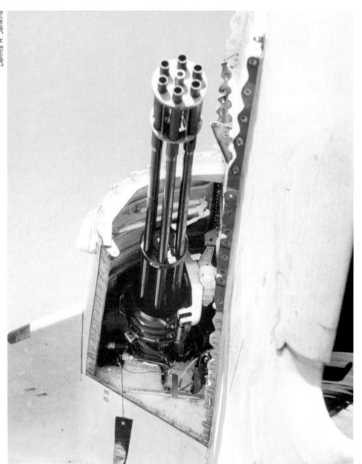

Most of the M61A1 is accessible when the lower and front access covers are removed. The M61A1 is hydraulically driven and weighs 275 lbs. A total of 940 rounds of ammunition are carried by all variants except the F-15E which carries 450 rounds. Surprisingly, the gun placement does not present any stability problems when it is firing.

F-15A INTERNAL GUN

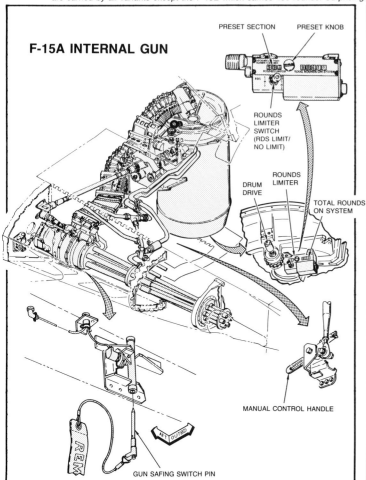

PRESET SECTION
PRESET KNOB

ROUNDS LIMITER SWITCH (RDS LIMIT/ NO LIMIT)

DRUM DRIVE

ROUNDS LIMITER

TOTAL ROUNDS ON SYSTEM

MANUAL CONTROL HANDLE

GUN SAFING SWITCH PIN

AFT OUTBD

F-15A EXTERNAL STORES LIMITATIONS

SUSPENSION EQUIPMENT

Suspension (Store)	Weight lb	9	8	7	6	5	4	3	2	1
LAU-106/A Launcher	50			1	1		1	1		
SUU-59/A Pylon*	345		1						1	
ADU-407/A Adapter (Launcher)	26		1						1	
LAU-114/A Launcher	51		1						1	
AERO-3B Launcher	49		1						1	
SUU-60/A Pylon*	296					1				
MER-200P Ejector Rack	500		1			1			1	
SUU-20B/A Dispenser (Empty)	276		1			1			1	
SUU-61/A Pylon (ECM)	50	1								1
MAU-12C/A Bomb Rack	81		1			1			1	

*Weight includes MAU-12C/A Bomb Rack

WEIGHTS INCLUDE SUSPENSION EQUIPMENT

STORE	LINE NUMBER	STATION LOADING AND SUSPENSION					MAXIMUM KCAS OR IMN WHICHEVER IS LESS			ACCELERATION-G				MAX DIVE FOR DEL	STORES CONFIGURATION WEIGHT LBS	DRAG INDEX	REMARKS
		1	2	5	8	9	CARRIAGE	EMPLOY-MENT	JETTISON	CARRIAGE SYM	UNSYM	EMPLOY-MENT	JETTISON				
AN/ALQ 119 V-12 Tews Pod	1			●			BAL	NA	NA	BAL	BAL	NA	NA	NA	876	6.7	● Jettison of Tews Pod is prohibited. Tews pods may be carried asymmetrically on either station 2 or 8. ● Tews pods cannot be operated on stations 2 & 8. ● Carriage of AN/ALQ 119(V)-12 Tews Pod is cleared only for aircraft in block 13 and up or with TCTO 1F-15A-852 accomplished and with SSU-60/A pylon modified by TCTO 16WG-25-501.
600 Gallon Fuel Tank and AN/ALQ 119(V)-12 Tews Pod	2		○	●	○		660 1.5		150 to 660 1.5				0.5 to 2.0		EMPTY 2186 FULL 10,116	22.1	**Below 15,000 feet MSL. **Tanks only.
	3	●	○	●	○	●	*450 660 1.5			0.0 to 3.0	0.0 to 3.0			**	EMPTY 2446 FULL 6411	21.1	***Rolls are restricted to a maximum of 1/2 lateral stick.
AIM-9J Missile	4		▦		▦		BAL	BAL	150 to 1.0 *	BAL	BAL	BAL	+0.5 to +2.0 *	NA	1662	16.8	● Subtract 870 pounds from stores configuration weight and 4.8 from total drag index if AIM-9J missiles are loaded with other inboard pylon mounted stores. ● USAF approved decron cont fix is mandatory to preclude roll-eron uncaging during captive carriage of AIM-9J. ● Use Aero-3B-, 9J, P.N. 7132809-30, launchers only. ● Only MK8, MOD 4 & 8 Clamp warheads (Live-Part Number 7531164; Inert--Part Number 7653446-10) may be installed. ★ Jettison limits pertain to proof jettison only.
AIM-7F Missile	5	MISSILE STATIONS					BAL	150 to 800 2.3	150 to 1.0	BAL	BAL	-0.5 to +7.33	+0.5 to +3.0	NA	2040	8.4	● Jettisoning of missiles permitted only between 250-350 knots, IG when tanks or AG weapons are carried on stations 2 & 8. ● Carriage of the AIM-7F LCDM is authorized to the same limits as identified above for live missiles providing the LCDM inspection has been accomplished in accordance with SPO directive dated 18 September 1974. ● Carriage of DUMMY TRAINING missiles is prohibited. **CAUTION** ● With AG weapons or wing tanks on stations 2 & 8, employment of AIM-7 missiles may result in missile impact with store or tank if within the following parameters: ● a. At or below 1G at any altitude or airspeed. ● b. At or below 2G if below 18,000 ft and above 466 KCAS. ● The aft missile will not be completely free of possible wing store interference until approximately 1.5 seconds after weapon release button depression.
		3	4	6	7												
	FWD	▦			▦												
	AFT		▦	▦													

NA — NOT APPLICABLE
NE — NOT ESTABLISHED
BAL — BASIC AIRCRAFT LIMITS

NOTES
● Speeds may be further limited by applicable aircraft/engine airspeed envelope.
● AN/ASQ-T10 POD, AIM-9J and AIM-7F missiles may be carried in conjection with any combination of stores loading on stations 2, 5, and 8.

Left table

WEIGHTS INCLUDE SUSPENSION EQUIPMENT

NA – NOT APPLICABLE
NE – NOT ESTABLISHED
BAL – BASIC AIRCRAFT LIMITS

STORE	LINE NUMBER	STATION LOADING AND SUSPENSION					MAXIMUM KCAS OR IMN WHICHEVER IS LESS			ACCELERATION-G				MAX DIVE FOR DEL	STORES CONFIGURATION WEIGHT LB	DRAG INDEX	REMARKS
		1	2	5	8	9	CARRIAGE	EMPLOY-MENT	JETTISON	CARRIAGE SYM	CARRIAGE UNSYM	EMPLOY-MENT	JETTISON				
MK 84 LDGP Bomb	1		●	●	●		600 1.4	600 1.4	150 to 600 1.4	BAL **	BAL		+0.5 to +7.33	+0.5 to +2.0	60°	6876	14.4	● Rolls at less than 0.06 above 600 Knots are prohibited. ● Unless all tanks are empty, roll rate is restricted to 120 degrees per second. Centerline tank only , unless empty, is restricted to 120 degrees per second, but only above Mach 1.0 ● Simultaneous (emergency or combat) jettison of wing tanks is prohibited above 800 KCAS. ● ** –2.0G above Mach 1.0.
600 Gallon Fuel Tank and MK 84 LDGP Bomb	2	○	●	○												EMPTY 3676 FULL 11,506	20.2	
	3		●	○												EMPTY 5226 FULL 9191	17.3	
MK 84 EO Bomb (GBU-8/B)	4		●	●	●		500 0.9	500 0.9	150 to 500 0.9	–2.0 to +5.0	–1.0 to +4.0		+0.5 to +5.0			7845	28.2	
600 Gallon Fuel Tank and MK 84 EO Bomb (GBU-8/B)	5	○	●	○												EMPTY 3899 FULL 11,829	24.8	
	6		●	○												EMPTY 5872 FULL 9837	26.5	
MK 84 LG Bomb (GBU-10A/B)	7		●	●	●		600 1.2	600 1.2	150 to 600 1.2							7125	28.2	
600 Gallon Fuel Tank and MK 84 LG Bomb (GBU-10A/B)	8	○	●	○												EMPTY 3659 FULL 11,589	24.8	
	9		●	○												EMPTY 5392 FULL 9357	26.5	
AN/ASQ-T10 Pod	10	●+●			●+●		BAL	NA	150 to 1.0 *	BAL	BAL	NA	+0.5 to +2.0 *			1638	16.8	● Carriage of any combination of pods alone or pods and missiles on stations 2 and 8 is permitted. * Jettison limits pertain to pylon jettison only.

Right table

WEIGHTS INCLUDE SUSPENSION EQUIPMENT

NA – NOT APPLICABLE
NE – NOT ESTABLISHED
BAL – BASIC AIRCRAFT LIMITS

STORE	LINE NUMBER	STATION LOADING AND SUSPENSION					MAXIMUM KCAS OR IMN WHICHEVER IS LESS			ACCELERATION-G				MAX DIVE FOR DEL	STORES CONFIGURATION WEIGHT LB	DRAG INDEX	REMARKS
		1	2	5	8	9	CARRIAGE	EMPLOY-MENT	JETTISON	CARRIAGE SYM	CARRIAGE UNSYM	EMPLOY-MENT	JETTISON				
600 Gallon Fuel Tank	1	○	○	○			600 1.5	NA	150 to 600 1.5	BAL **	NA	NA	+2.0	NA	EMPTY 1926 FULL 13,821	23.1	● Unless all tanks are empty, roll rate is restricted to 120 degrees per second. Centerline tank only , unless empty, is restricted to 120 degrees per second, but only above Mach 1.0 ● Simultaneous (emergency or combat) jettison of wing tanks is prohibited above 800 KCAS. ● With any combination of external tanks installed, rolls at less than zero G's are prohibited above 800 KCAS. * Jettison of SUU-20B/A Dispenser permitted only with pylon attached. ** –2.0G above Mach 1.0.
	2	○		○											EMPTY 1310 FULL 9240	15.4	
	3			○											EMPTY 616 FULL 4581	7.7	
SUU-60/A C Pylon	4			●			BAL	NA	150 to 700 1.4	BAL	BAL	NA	+0.5 to +2.0	NA	296	2.4	
SUU-59/A Inboard Pylon	5	●		●			BAL	NA	150 to 600 1.4	BAL	BAL	NA	+0.5 to +2.0	NA	670	4.8	
SUU-20B/A Dispenser	6	●	●	●	●		700 2.0	250 to 520 1.0	150 to 1.0 *	BAL **	BAL	0.0 to +5.00	+0.5 to +2.0 *	60°	E1794 F2220	E18.0 F16.2	
	7	●	●	●	●										E1222 F1606	E12.0 F10.8	
	8		●												E572 F714	E6.0 F5.4	
600 Gallon Fuel Tank and SUU-20B/A Dispenser	9	●	○	●	○		600 1.5	250 to 520 1.0	150 to 1.0 *	BAL **	BAL	0.0 to +5.00	+0.5 to +2.0 *	60° Tanks 60° SUU-20B/A	EMPTY 1838 FULL 8007	E19.7 F18.5	
	10	○	●	○											EMPTY 1882 FULL 9054	E21.4 F20.8	

The rails for AIM-9 and/or AIM-120A missiles are located mid-way up the inboard wing pylons. No other weapons are cleared for carriage on these locations.

George Cockle

As the inboard wing pylons create little additional drag they are usually left on the aircraft at all times. Outboard wing pylons are not cleared to carry any stores.

George Cockle

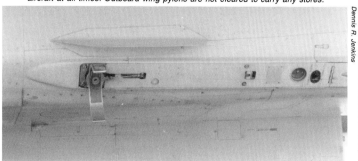

The aft AIM-7 station shows attachment points and the small strakes used to ensure clean missile separation. The fuselage stations are also capable of carrying AIM-120As.

Dennis R. Jenkins

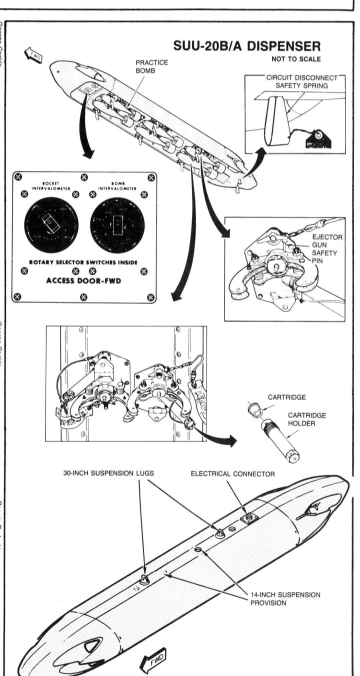

SUU-20B/A DISPENSER

NOT TO SCALE

PRACTICE BOMB

CIRCUIT DISCONNECT SAFETY SPRING

ROCKET INTERVALOMETER

BOMB INTERVALOMETER

ROTARY SELECTOR SWITCHES INSIDE

ACCESS DOOR-FWD

EJECTOR GUN SAFETY PIN

CARTRIDGE

CARTRIDGE HOLDER

30-INCH SUSPENSION LUGS

ELECTRICAL CONNECTOR

14-INCH SUSPENSION PROVISION

FWD

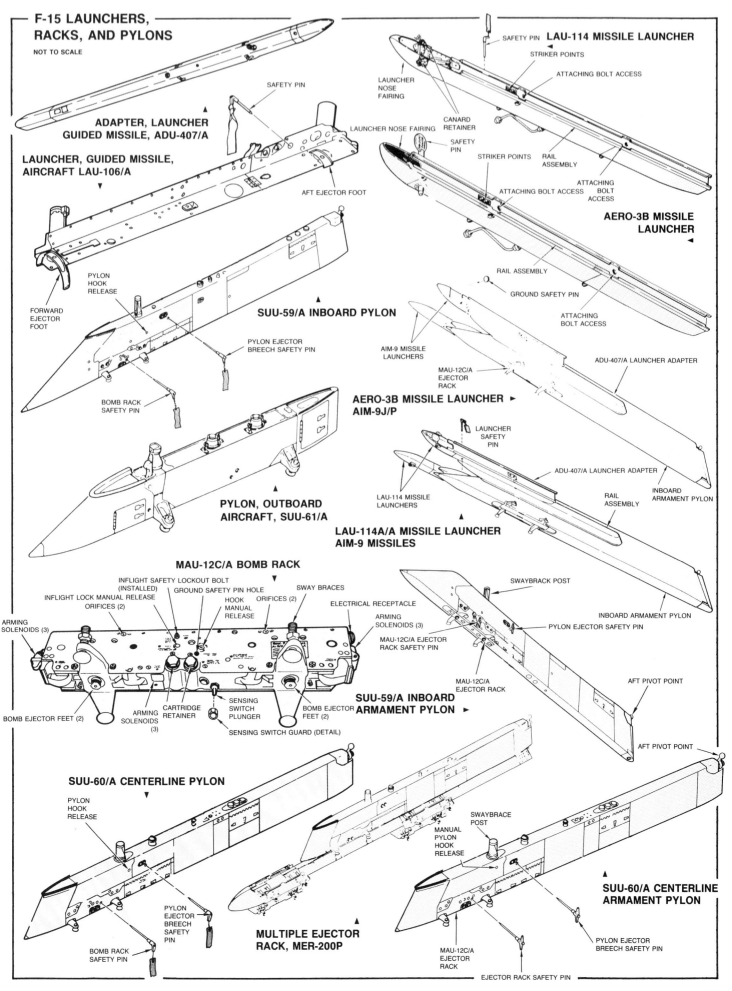

F-15 LAUNCHERS, RACKS, AND PYLONS

NOT TO SCALE

SAFETY PIN

ADAPTER, LAUNCHER GUIDED MISSILE, ADU-407/A ▲

LAUNCHER, GUIDED MISSILE, AIRCRAFT LAU-106/A ▼

SAFETY PIN

AFT EJECTOR FOOT

PYLON HOOK RELEASE

FORWARD EJECTOR FOOT

SUU-59/A INBOARD PYLON ▲

PYLON EJECTOR BREECH SAFETY PIN

BOMB RACK SAFETY PIN

PYLON, OUTBOARD AIRCRAFT, SUU-61/A ▲

MAU-12C/A BOMB RACK ▼

INFLIGHT SAFETY LOCKOUT BOLT (INSTALLED)
INFLIGHT LOCK MANUAL RELEASE ORIFICES (2)
GROUND SAFETY PIN HOLE
HOOK MANUAL RELEASE
ORIFICES (2)
SWAY BRACES
ELECTRICAL RECEPTACLE
ARMING SOLENOIDS (3)

ARMING SOLENOIDS (3)

BOMB EJECTOR FEET (2)
ARMING SOLENOIDS (3)
CARTRIDGE RETAINER
SENSING SWITCH PLUNGER
SENSING SWITCH GUARD (DETAIL)
BOMB EJECTOR FEET (2)

SUU-60/A CENTERLINE PYLON ▼

PYLON HOOK RELEASE

PYLON EJECTOR BREECH SAFETY PIN

BOMB RACK SAFETY PIN

MULTIPLE EJECTOR RACK, MER-200P ▼

SAFETY PIN LAU-114 MISSILE LAUNCHER ◄
STRIKER POINTS
ATTACHING BOLT ACCESS

LAUNCHER NOSE FAIRING

CANARD RETAINER
SAFETY PIN

LAUNCHER NOSE FAIRING
STRIKER POINTS
RAIL ASSEMBLY
ATTACHING BOLT ACCESS
ATTACHING BOLT ACCESS

AERO-3B MISSILE LAUNCHER ◄

RAIL ASSEMBLY
GROUND SAFETY PIN
ATTACHING BOLT ACCESS

AIM-9 MISSILE LAUNCHERS
MAU-12C/A EJECTOR RACK

ADU-407/A LAUNCHER ADAPTER

AERO-3B MISSILE LAUNCHER ► AIM-9J/P

LAUNCHER SAFETY PIN

LAU-114 MISSILE LAUNCHERS

ADU-407/A LAUNCHER ADAPTER

RAIL ASSEMBLY

INBOARD ARMAMENT PYLON

LAU-114A/A MISSILE LAUNCHER ▲ AIM-9 MISSILES

SWAYBRACK POST

INBOARD ARMAMENT PYLON
PYLON EJECTOR SAFETY PIN

MAU-12C/A EJECTOR RACK SAFETY PIN

MAU-12C/A EJECTOR RACK

AFT PIVOT POINT

SUU-59/A INBOARD ARMAMENT PYLON ►

AFT PIVOT POINT

SWAYBRACE POST

MANUAL PYLON HOOK RELEASE

SUU-60/A CENTERLINE ARMAMENT PYLON ▲

MAU-12C/A EJECTOR RACK

PYLON EJECTOR BREECH SAFETY PIN

EJECTOR RACK SAFETY PIN

When only one AIM-9 is carried it is generally carried on the outboard rail, while single AIM-7s are generally carried on the forward fuselage station.

The F-15 is capable of carrying several versions of the venerable AIM-9 "Sidewinder" short-range air-to-air missile which has the highest kill-probability of any U.S. AAM.

Distinctive leading edge break in canard design identifieds the AIM-9L. Navy utilized similar AIM-9M, but all other "Sidewinder" version were considerably different. The AIM-9L has all-aspect acquisition and intercept capabilities against highly maneuvering, high-speed targets.

Two F-15As (76-0086 and 77-0084) were modified to carry the Vought Anti-Satellite (ASAT) missile on their centerline pylons. This missile used a miniature-homing vehicle warhead that actually destroyed its target with kinetic energy. The first intercept launch was made on September 13, 1985 against the Solwind P78-1 satellite.

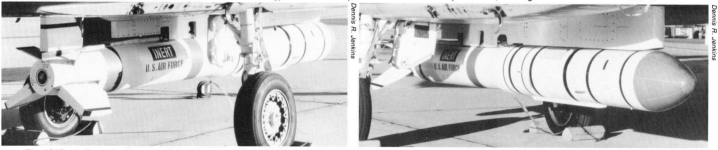

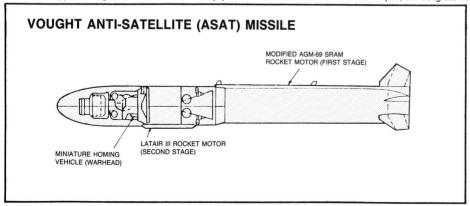

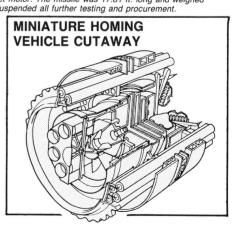

The ASAT missile used a first stage derived from an AGM-69 SRAM and a second stage powered by an Altair III rocket motor. The missile was 17.81 ft. long and weighed approximately 2,700 lbs. Plans were to equip the 48th FIS and 318th FIS with the weapon, but Congress has suspended all further testing and procurement.

VOUGHT ANTI-SATELLITE (ASAT) MISSILE

MODIFIED AGM-69 SRAM
ROCKET MOTOR (FIRST STAGE)

LATAIR III ROCKET MOTOR
(SECOND STAGE)

MINIATURE HOMING
VEHICLE (WARHEAD)

MINIATURE HOMING VEHICLE CUTAWAY

The second F-15B (71-291) carries B61 nuclear weapons on the inboard wing pylons and centerline. Only the F-15E is currently certified to carry tactical nuclear weapons.

The first F-15C (78-0468) carries a B61 nuclear weapon suspended from the MER attach-point on each type-1 CFT and a 610 gal. fuel tank on each wing pylon.

The original ground-attack load was to be carried on 5 MERs (each CFT, each wing, and centerline) as shown at left. This configuration created excessive drag, leading to the development of the type-4 CFT equipped for low-drag tangential carriage of weapons (right) for the F-15E. The AIM-120A on the inboard rail at right is noteworthy.

The Hughes AIM-120A AMRAAM is scheduled to replace both the AIM-7 and AIM-9 during the 1990s. The missile is capable of rail-launching (shown) and drop-launching. There have been some vibration/flutter problems when carried on the F-15's forward AIM-7 station. The 33rd TFW at Eglin will be the first unit to receive AMRAAMs during late 1989.

The first F-15C shows a mix of regular (on wing pylon) and high-drag (on CFT) Mk82 500 lb. bombs. The MER-200 racks used by the F-15 are of an improved design.

Early brass-board guidance hardware for the AIM-120A AMRAAM was flight tested in a modified 610 gal. external fuel tank. Note cooling air scoop under rear of tank.

Dennis R. Jenkins

Dennis R. Jenkins

The first F-15E (86-0183) with early type-1 conformal fuel tanks, LANTIRN pods, AIM-7s on the CFT stations, AIM-9s and 2,000 lb. laser-guided bombs on the wing pylons.

The F-15E has small pylons under each air intake for the Martin Marietta LANTIRN navigation and targeting pods. Notice molded plastic intake FOD shield.

Dennis R. Jenkins

Dennis R. Jenkins

The Westinghouse AN/ALQ-119(V) TEWS pod was originally to be carried on the outer wing pylons but flutter problems dictated carriage on the centerline only.

Late F-15Cs and all F-15Es introduced an AN/ALQ-135 antenna on the right fuselage extension immediately aft of the vertical stabilizer to provide tail warning coverage.

McDonnell Douglas

McDonnell Douglas developed a conformal reconnaissance pod that can be carried on the F-15's centerline station. This pod was successfully tested on 71-291 during the Reconnaissance Technology Demonstrator program. The pod carried forward oblique, vertical, and side oblique film cameras as well as an infrared camera.

STORE PHYSICAL CHARACTERISTICS
(F-15 SPECIFIED STORES)

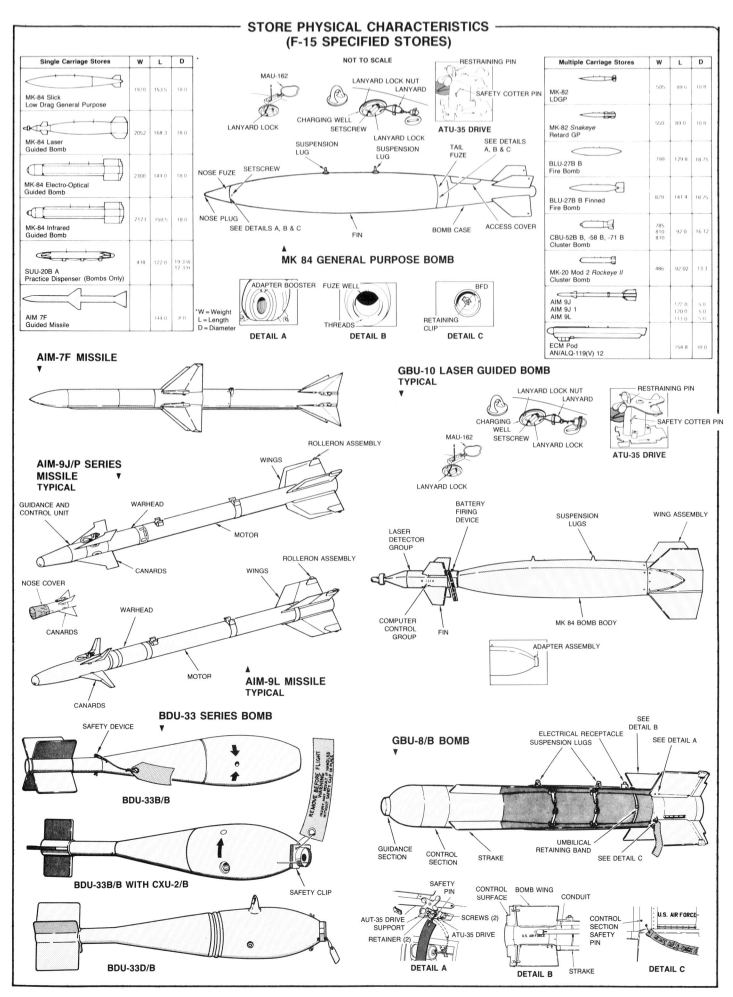

Single Carriage Stores	W	L	D*
MK-84 Slick Low Drag General Purpose	1970	153.5	18.0
MK-84 Laser Guided Bomb	2052	168.3	18.0
MK-84 Electro-Optical Guided Bomb	2300	149.0	18.0
MK-84 Infrared Guided Bomb	2123	150.5	18.0
SUU-20B A Practice Dispenser (Bombs Only)	418	122.0	19.3 W 12.3 H
AIM 7F Guided Missile		144.0	8.0

*W = Weight L = Length D = Diameter

Multiple Carriage Stores	W	L	D
MK-82 LDGP	505	89.6	10.8
MK-82 *Snakeye* Retard GP	550	89.0	10.8
BLU-27B B Fire Bomb	799	129.8	18.75
BLU-27B B Finned Fire Bomb	829	141.4	18.75
CBU-52B B, -58 B, -71 B Cluster Bomb	785 810 810	92.0	16.12
MK-20 Mod 2 *Rockeye II* Cluster Bomb	486	92.02	13.3
AIM 9J AIM 9J 1 AIM 9L		122.0 120.0 111.0	5.0 5.0 5.0
ECM Pod AN/ALQ-119(V) 12		154.8	10.0

NOT TO SCALE

MAU-162 · LANYARD LOCK · CHARGING WELL SETSCREW · LANYARD LOCK NUT LANYARD · LANYARD LOCK · RESTRAINING PIN · SAFETY COTTER PIN · ATU-35 DRIVE

SUSPENSION LUG · SUSPENSION LUG · TAIL FUZE · SEE DETAILS A, B & C · NOSE FUZE · SETSCREW · NOSE PLUG · SEE DETAILS A, B & C · FIN · BOMB CASE · ACCESS COVER

MK 84 GENERAL PURPOSE BOMB

ADAPTER BOOSTER · FUZE WELL · BFD · THREADS · RETAINING CLIP

DETAIL A   DETAIL B   DETAIL C

AIM-7F MISSILE

AIM-9J/P SERIES MISSILE TYPICAL
ROLLERON ASSEMBLY · WINGS · GUIDANCE AND CONTROL UNIT · WARHEAD · MOTOR · CANARDS · NOSE COVER · CANARDS · WARHEAD · WINGS · ROLLERON ASSEMBLY

AIM-9L MISSILE TYPICAL
MOTOR · CANARDS

BDU-33 SERIES BOMB
SAFETY DEVICE · BDU-33B/B · REMOVE BEFORE FLIGHT · BDU-33B/B WITH CXU-2/B · SAFETY CLIP · BDU-33D/B

GBU-10 LASER GUIDED BOMB TYPICAL
LANYARD LOCK NUT LANYARD · RESTRAINING PIN · CHARGING WELL SETSCREW · MAU-162 · LANYARD LOCK · SAFETY COTTER PIN · LANYARD LOCK · ATU-35 DRIVE

BATTERY FIRING DEVICE · SUSPENSION LUGS · WING ASSEMBLY · LASER DETECTOR GROUP · COMPUTER CONTROL GROUP · FIN · MK 84 BOMB BODY · ADAPTER ASSEMBLY

GBU-8/B BOMB
SEE DETAIL B · ELECTRICAL RECEPTACLE SUSPENSION LUGS · SEE DETAIL A · GUIDANCE SECTION · CONTROL SECTION · STRAKE · UMBILICAL RETAINING BAND · SEE DETAIL C · SAFETY PIN · CONTROL SURFACE · BOMB WING · CONDUIT · CONTROL SECTION SAFETY PIN · U.S. AIR FORCE · AUT-35 DRIVE SUPPORT · SCREWS (2) · ATU-35 DRIVE · RETAINER (2) · STRAKE

DETAIL A   DETAIL B   DETAIL C

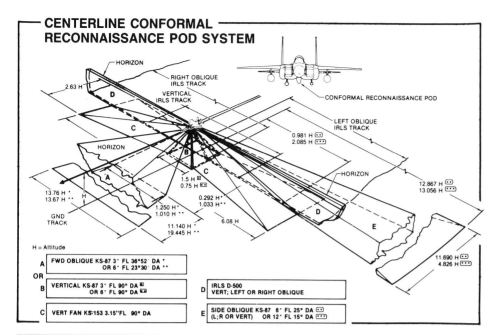

CENTERLINE CONFORMAL RECONNAISSANCE POD SYSTEM

HORIZON

RIGHT OBLIQUE IRLS TRACK

VERTICAL IRLS TRACK

2.63 H

CONFORMAL RECONNAISSANCE POD

LEFT OBLIQUE IRLS TRACK

0.981 H
2.085 H

HORIZON

HORIZON

12.867 H
13.056 H

1.5 H
0.75 H

13.76 H *
13.67 H **

GND TRACK

0.292 H *
1.033 H **

1.250 H *
1.010 H **

11.690 H
4.826 H

11.140 H *
19.445 H **

6.08 H

H = Altitude

A	FWD OBLIQUE KS-87 3″ FL 36°52′ DA * OR 6″ FL 23°30′ DA **
OR	
B	VERTICAL KS-87 3″ FL 90° DA OR 6″ FL 90° DA
C	VERT FAN KS-153 3.15″FL 90° DA

D	IRLS D-500 VERT; LEFT OR RIGHT OBLIQUE
E	SIDE OBLIQUE KS-87 6″ FL 25° DA (L;R OR VERT) OR 12″ FL 15° DA

George Cockle

George Cockle

George Cockle

Travel pods can be carried on the inboard wing stations and the centerline. On single-seaters one is normally carried on the left wing station for cross-country flights, while two-seaters generally carry one on each wing.

Typical F-15 flight gear includes g-suit and survival vest. Inflation is controlled by onboard system.

F-15E:

McDonnell Douglas

Dennis Jenkins

Front cockpit of F-15E, 86-0184. Digitized and CRT-type presentations predominate. Only minimal analog instrumentation is provided. CRTs are surrounded by push-buttons for data call-up.

Left console of F-15E front cockpit serves as mounting point for dual-handle throttle quadrant.

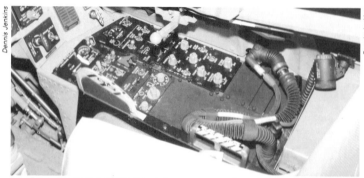

Right console of F-15E front cockpit serves as mounting point for environmental, lighting, and other miscellaneous controls.

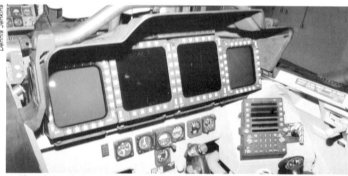

Aft cockpit main instrument panel is dominated by four large CRTs. Digitized enunciator panel is visible on right. Note small complement of analog instrumentation.

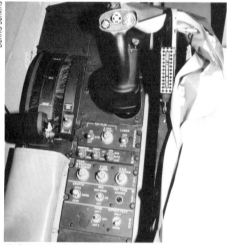

Left console of aft cockpit serves as mounting point for sensor systems side stick controller and throttle.

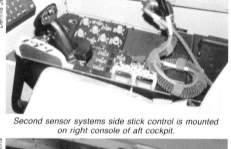

Second sensor systems side stick control is mounted on right console of aft cockpit.

Aft view of F-15E canopy in raised position. Basic canopy consists of two sections of acrylic laminate.

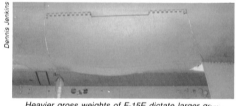

Heavier gross weights of F-15E dictate larger gear. These require a slight bulge to main gear doors.

Main gear of F-15E are strengthened to accommodate increased gross takeoff weight of "Strike Eagle".

Doppler antenna fairing is mounted near aircraft centerline between engine nacelle fairings.

Inflight refueling receptacle is mounted in wing root fairing. White outline improves visibility at night.

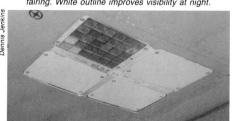

Chaff dispenser is built into fuselage underside and is equipped with 30 compartments.

Like main gear, F-15E nose gear also has been given extra strength and increased wheel and tire load.

Wheel and brake design is subtly different from that found on earlier, lighter F-15 models.

AN/AAQ-13 has been assigned to the starboard nacelle pylon assembly. Additional pylons are mounted on the conformal fuel tanks. Gun port is visible in wing root fairing.

Conformal tank fairs neatly under empennage chine and engine nacelle section. No less than four conformal racks are attached to this unit.

Hughes AN/APG-70 radar is optimized for use in the F-15E. Planar antenna is equipped with ten dipoles mounted near its periphery.

AN/AAQ-13 is always carried on starboard pylon. Unit is optimized to provide forward looking infrared imagery.

F-15E, 87-0183, of the 4th TFW, Seymour Johnson AFB, S. Carolina. This was the first operational "Strike Eagle". AN/AAQ-13 and AN/AAQ-14 pods are readily discernible.

AGM-65 "Maverick" can be accommodated on F-15E wing stations only. Visible under fuselage are AN/AAQ-13 and AN/AAQ-14 pods.

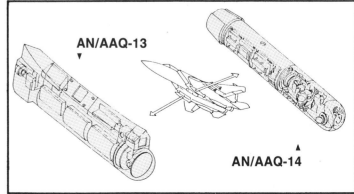

AN/AAQ-13

AN/AAQ-14